Contents

Dedication

For Daniel.

Introduction

The issues of quality and service are the major management concerns for all organisations in the 1990s. Industry and commerce in Britain have already started addressing them and awareness is increasing in the public sector, notably the NHS and local government.

This book assimilates and applies the lessons of the quality movement to schools. There is little in the book that is unique, it is rather a starting point, a contribution to the debate on how to ensure that schools provide the best possible learning opportunities for children. It is recognised that changes in the terminology of many of the chapters of this book would allow schools to claim that they already operate total quality management. This is not a problem. In fact it is essential that education does evolve its own view on how to manage quality.

Inevitably a book of this length can only highlight issues, but in doing so can demonstrate a contribution to the process of continuous improvement. It is very much hoped that readers will respond to the invitation in the review section in order to advance the debate.

A wide range of individuals and organisations have contributed, knowingly and unknowingly, to the writing of this book. To Joss and Daniel, for the loss of evenings and weekends, my love and thanks. Pat and Dave Lambert, Lyn Lambert and Jack Lindstrom provided quality thinking time, space and ideas. Kim Lewis of Ad hoc Systems Limited, Nottingham displayed an amazing ability to get it right first time and Roger Henwood of Longmans proved the most tolerant of customers.

Specific thanks must go to CRAC for organising the first significant course on TQM in education; to Jeff Prest of ICI, John Chesterton of ICL, Nick Massey of the co-operative Bank, Steve Hart of Profile Consulting and John Woodward of Q.Ed. all of whom gave freely of ideas and time. Steve Holman first introduced me to the key concepts of TQM. To all my thanks and the hope that I have done them justice.

Finally I acknowledge the many colleagues in Cheshire who have participated enthusiastically in courses where many of the ideas in this book have been explored and developed. To them my special thanks and the reassurance that the final responsibility is mine and mine alone. Equally the views expressed here are mine.

John West-Burnham

1 Why quality?

This chapter seeks to set the debate about quality in schools in context, and outline the particular approach adopted in this book. The fundamental assumption is that the changes facing schools following the 1988 Education Reform Act are so profound that traditional approaches to managing schools may no longer be appropriate and radical alternatives have to be considered. This chapter therefore explores:

- the changing context of school management;
- the drive for quality;
- total quality management;
- objections to the total quality approach;
- parallel developments.

The changing context of school management

The Education Acts of the 1980s provide the most fundamental challenge to the established ways of doing things in schools. The changes are so basic that it is doubtful that schools will survive unless their response to the changes is of the same order of magnitude as the changes themselves. Historically schools have responded to change in an incremental and piecemeal fashion, gradually assimilating some new requirements, subverting or modifying others and even ignoring a few. The realignment of the education service following the 1988 Education Act in particular makes such responses inappropriate and impractical. Indeed the lack of a coordinated response may well prove to be dysfunctional, not only generating acute internal tensions but questioning the survival of the school itself. The analogy may be drawn with the person planning to take up the game of squash: investing in designer clothing and equipment, reading the rule book and joining the club but not bothering to develop the skills or, crucially, to get fit. A heart attack often results; in order to get fit a diagnosis of the demands to be made on the system is necessary.

Readers will not need reminding of the range and complexity of the changes impinging on schools, however, it is worth itemising those components which pose the greatest challenge to established ways of working. These may be summarised as: the National Curriculum, LMS, appraisal, consumer rights and social pressures.

The National Curriculum

The key management issues may be identified as:

- managing time so as to meet all the requirements of the curriculum;
- developing resources in response to new demands;
- deploying staff to maximise available expertise;
- managing assessment procedures and recording achievement;
- developing staff in the new skills and knowledge;
- managing cross-curricular themes;
- implementing appropriate learning strategies;
- reporting academic outcomes.

Apart from these specific aspects the implications of these changes also have to be managed. Most significant of these are the demands on teacher time, e.g. the introduction of 'new' subjects and approaches to assessment in the primary school and the challenge to traditional ways of structuring learning in the secondary school. Therefore, to the operational issues must be added concerns about teacher stress, motivation and perceived challenges to traditional views of professional autonomy.

Local management of schools

The impact and implications of LMS are increasingly understood – the specific issues may be identified as:

- the changing role of the governing body;
- integrating budgeting, curriculum and staffing plans into a strategic approach;

- managing parental choice procedures;
- assuming full responsibility for staffing;
- establishing administrative procedures;
- marketing the school;
- responding to new reporting, inspection and audit requirements;
- reviewing senior management roles and responsibilities;
- managing a formula funded budget.

These factors have had the combined effect of requiring the implementation of a whole new range of procedures whilst potentially detracting from the core purpose of schools – the management of learning. They have confronted senior staff with stark choices and direct accountability for the implications of their actions. Issues related to job security and resource availability are now directly located in the school.

Appraisal

The full potential of the appraisal regulations for schools will not be understood for some time. However, the introduction of the process will raise a number of issues:

- the clarity of the school's values and purpose;
- the effectiveness of management processes;
- the credibility of managers as appraisers;
- the definition of criteria for effectiveness;
- the quality of personal relationships;
- the management of professional development;
- the use of appropriate personnel procedures in response to the range of performance issues.

It would be wrong to extol the potential benefits of a professional model of teacher appraisal without recognising the significant concerns it generates. The most common of these is the likely impact on time but there are also real concerns about observation, confidentiality and the use of appraisal data for purposes other than development.

Consumer rights

The introduction of a crypto-consumerism under LMS is likely to become more overt in response to citizens' and parents' charters. Possible implications of this approach might include:

- financial penalties and rewards linked to performance;
- increased demands for information;
- publication of comparative data;
- greater accessibility to school procedures.

Few teachers will object in principle to the notion that their customers should have the same rights as they enjoy as consumers. However, there is a substantial difference between complaining about a badly serviced car and complaints about literacy rates or GCSE results. The principle is the same but the measures to be applied and the variables operating are very different.

Social pressures

This is the least tangible of the factors impinging on school management in the 1990s but will be a vital determinant of quality. Unemployment, social disadvantage, domestic stress and cultural deprivation are all issues which act as crucial determinants on the ways in which schools are managed. The more acute the problems of the environment in which a school has to function the greater the demands on the skills and qualities of teachers and the fewer the resources likely to be available. If the factors outlined above are added to the social pressures under which many schools operate then the challenge to leaders and managers is profound.

To these pressures must be added increased competition between LEA maintained schools, the independent sector, grant maintained schools and city technology colleges. The equation is further complicated by changes in 16–19 provision and higher education as well as changes in the expectations of employers.

The combination of these factors poses the most significant challenge to the prevailing orthodoxies of the theory and practice of school management. The first response is that schools have to be managed by professionals who have the knowledge, skills and qualities appropriate to the new situation. Schools that deny the importance of planning, budget management and the deployment and development of staff in the context of curriculum leadership are putting a question mark over their survival. There is a need to develop a coherent and systematic view of what the management of learning in schools means. Symptomatic of the problem are the following aspects of school management:

- no clear or agreed criteria as to the components of school management;
- unclear definitions of the purposes of senior and middle management;

- deference to experience over skills and qualities;
- limited access to management – the word is used as a collective noun rather than to describe a process;
- training is often random, ad-hoc and peripheral;
- administrative procedures are seen as a substitute for effective management;
- management as a process lacks a focus on learning.

The net effect of these elements is the danger that managerialism, i.e. procedures carried out for their own sake will come to be regarded as managing. This will inevitably detract from the key purpose of schools and elevate concern for power, status and systems to the detriment of facilitating effective learning. Bureaucratic responses to complexity are always the easiest.

This problem is not unique to the education service. Many commercial, industrial and public sector organisations are facing a choice in responding to complex change: either become more formal and structured or adopt a radical and fundamental alternative. For many that alternative is total quality management.

The drive for quality

For the cynical, quality is the management 'flavour of the decade', a fashion, a bandwagon which in time will be replaced by another set of prescriptions. Formulations as to the 'correct approaches' undoubtedly change but it is possible to be more confident about the quality movement for two reasons. Firstly, it has been around for 40 years – it is not a passing whim, it has taken a long time to percolate through the literature. Secondly, however quality is defined, it has always been at the centre of the debate about education. There are few other social processes where a concern for standards has been such a constant imperative. As has been argued above, the 1988 Education Reform Act highlights and reinforces this concern – to this must be added a range of other driving forces. Sallis (1991) has identified four imperatives for introducing TQM, the professional, the moral, the competitive and survival. These are identified in the context of further education, however, they are equally valid for schools. Changing the language to match the situation facing schools the following reasons may be identified for adopting a quality management approach:

1. The moral imperative

If schools are about anything then they have to be fundamentally and obsessively concerned with providing children with the very best educational opportunities possible. It is difficult to conceptualise a situation where anything less than total quality is perceived as being appropriate or acceptable for the education of children. The moral imperative is concerned with optimising the opportunities for children to achieve their full potential so that their years of compulsory education culminate in the maximum appropriate outcomes. This places an enormous burden of responsibility on teachers and managers in schools to enhance every opportunity for the growth and development of children. This in turn requires that values are at the core of every decision making process and educational procedure.

The moral imperative is very closely related to the professional imperative in that professionalism implies a commitment to the needs of a client and an obligation to meet those needs by deploying knowledge and skills to best effect. Being a professional confers a moral imperative to deliver consistent high levels of service. Crucially this applies as much to managing the school as to managing the classroom.

2. The environmental imperative

Schools are in a dynamic interaction with the society and community which they serve. That environment is becoming increasingly quality conscious. If schools are to be genuinely responsive then they increasingly need to be aware of, and respond to, quality issues. Further and higher education, employers and other external agencies are using the vocabulary and processes of quality. Pupils leaving schools will go to work in TQM businesses, continue their studies in colleges with quality systems and, most importantly, go home to parents who are increasingly aware of their rights as citizens and consumers. Most schools have as part of their aims the 'preparation of pupils for work, continuing education and citizenship'. If this is to be a genuine experience rather than didactic imperative then schools will need to assimilate the vocabulary and processes of quality.

Just as significant is the fact that as schools become increasingly autonomous in their dealings with external agencies, suppliers etc., so they should become more articulate in demanding quality service.

3. The survival imperative

The pressures of LMS raise the very real possibilities of compulsory redundancy and school closure. In simplistic terms enrolments will fall and schools will cease to be viable if they fail to satisfy customer needs and expectations. The customer driven approach of TQM is therefore a pragmatic response to ensuring continuing recruitment of pupils.

However, this does not imply a desperate attempt at cloning that which is perceived to be 'best school', rather a genuine responsiveness to the specific community in which a school is located. One of the imperatives facing senior managers in schools is the survival of the school. Parental satisfaction is one of the key determinants of a school's viability, TQM provides a powerful mechanism for ensuring consistency of response.

4. The accountability imperative

The increasing emphasis on the inspection and reporting of schools requires the development of internal strategies to generate appropriate data and processes which will accommodate and incorporate reporting and inspection procedures. TQM provides the vehicle for making these procedures intrinsic to school management processes and ensuring an effective response. If reporting and inspection are seen as ways of responding to customer requirements then they will become implicit to school processes rather than an 'alien' activity.

The net results of these imperatives is that schools will have to see themselves as part of their communities, not in the sense of identifying and providing services *they* consider appropriate but rather meeting the needs and requirements as specified by that community. Total quality management provides an integrated response which has the potential to meet the demands of these imperatives in a manner which is consistent with the special nature of schools as organisations.

Total quality management

Detailed definitions of TQM are developed in Chapter 2 and applied throughout the rest of this book. However, it is appropriate at this stage to introduce its key components to demonstrate how it meets the needs identified so far in this chapter. The key principles of TQM may be summarised as shown in Figure 1.1

FOCUS	Internal and External Customers
DEFINITION	Meeting Customer Requirements
SCOPE	Every Aspect of the Organisation
RESPONSIBILITY	Everyone
STANDARD	Right First Time - Fitness for Purpose
METHOD	Prevention not Detection
MEASUREMENT	Zero Defects
CULTURE	Continuous Improvement

Figure 1.1 Defining total quality management

These basic points are elaborated throughout this book, however, it is worth stressing at this stage that TQM organisations are about much more than responding to clients. They are as much about creativity, team-work, celebration, growth, recognition and excitement as creating effective processes. This is why this book argues that TQM is particularly appropriate for schools. TQM will not work if it is perceived as a series of mechanistic processes. Above everything else it is about the quality of personal relationships and this is an area where schools should have a significant advantage.

Equally significantly TQM is about survival, it is a means for ensuring that a particular organisation is the natural 'first choice' for its potential customers. Every reader will be aware of having made deliberate choices to buy or not buy a particular product or service on the basis of personal satisfaction or dissatisfaction. The central determinant in returning to a shop, a garage, a restaurant or holiday resort is most likely to be the extent to which needs were met and the way they were met. The choices which teachers apply in their own social and economic lives are now available to their customers.

TQM therefore provides an approach to managing schools which is sufficiently pragmatic to meet the changing environment that schools are having to operate in whilst being centrally and fundamentally concerned with values and moral considerations. However it would be naive to imagine that a system originated by American engineers and developed in Japanese mass production companies will automatically commend itself to British teachers.

Objections to the total quality approach

Everard and Morris (1990) provide a useful and succinct summary of a number of objections to the notion of management in education. The objections are largely academic and in many cases have been overtaken by events, i.e. schools have to be managed in order to survive. However, pragmatism does not guarantee appropriate styles of management. The main objections may be summarised as follows:

1. Managerialism denies professionalism.
2. Hierarchical accountability diminishes collegiality and autonomy.
3. The emphasis on leadership denies democracy.
4. Managerialism denies educational values.
5. Management is inevitably manipulative.
6. Educational outcomes cannot be managed.

It is difficult to respond to these concerns without challenging a fundamental misapprehension, i.e. the claimed definition of management. Many organisations would share the concerns identified above; most TQM companies would reject the implicit definitions of management as a power based, coercive, manipulative strategy which is cynically pragmatic as inappropriate and unacceptable. It will be for the reader to decide at the end of this book if the six objections are valid with respect to TQM. A central hypothesis of this study is that TQM is an appropriate model for schools because it does counter each objection.

There is every good reason for rejecting managerialism, i.e. management for its own sake where systems, status and routines take priority over real needs. TQM offers a value driven approach to management based on effective human relationships. Whilst educational outcomes may be intangible educational processes are not – they are based on the reality of day-to-day interactions in classrooms and staffrooms and these have to be managed. What is undeniable is that many schools which would reject the conceptual framework of TQM do in fact practise quality management. The labels are less significant than the content. Equally there are other initiatives which parallel the TQM movement but which are particular to schools.

Parallel developments

Two main initiatives may be identified which have the same concerns and many of the same outcomes as TQM: the 'effective schools' movement and school improvement. The research into effective schools has been usefully distilled by Hopkins (1987, p.3) where he identifies eight organisational factors which are characteristic of effective schools:

1. Curriculum-focused leadership.
2. Supportive climate.
3. Emphasis on learning.
4. Clear goals and high expectations.
5. Monitoring performance and achievement.
6. Continuous staff development.
7. Parental involvement.
8. LEA support.

Hopkins also stresses the importance of process factors in creating effective schools, quoting Fullan (1985) he identifies four factors:

1. Leadership as process rather than status.
2. An explicit value system which is consensual.
3. Sophisticated social interaction and communication.
4. Collaborative planning.

Slight changes in language and emphasis would allow these factors to be claimed by many TQM companies. The issue that is frequently not addressed in the educational literature is *how* to achieve these situations in practical terms.

The International School Improvement Project (ISIP) produced an important international perspective on the issues relevant to school improvement: the report produced a number of 'lessons' for schools in the United Kingdom:

1. Careful and accurate situational analysis.
2. Needs carefully identified.
3. Need for change clearly appreciated.
4. Carefully thought out strategy.
5. Strategy communicated effectively.
6. Changes reinforced and institutionalised.
7. Change supported and resourced.
   (Hopkins 1987, p.188).

The parallels with the principles for effectiveness and the definition of TQM in Figure 1.1 are clear. The links are reinforced in Chapter 9, most importantly in the notion of continuous improvement through development. Although its cultural pedigree is very different, TQM has many significant parallels with existing initiatives in education. What TQM has to offer is an holistic approach; an integrated view which incorporates structures, processes and relationships. However, there is no 'off the shelf package' no neat series of prescriptions. Although many TQM organisations have approaches in common and use similar language, the actual operation of TQM has to be unique; it must be created by the school in response to its own environment and through its own processes.

Summary

- The complexity of the changes facing schools requires radical changes to management styles.
- The key demands on schools may be identified as the National Curriculum, LMS, appraisal, consumer rights and social pressures.
- Traditional approaches to education management may no longer be appropriate.
- Quality is an increasingly significant issue for all organisations in Britain.
- Total quality management offers an appropriate response to the demands on schools and the need for a new management approach.
- The objections to management in schools are based on fundamental misapprehensions.
- TQM is compatible with other educational initiatives concerned with effectiveness and improvement.

Action

Establish the extent to which you are working in a quality school by completing the following diagnostic inventory. Compare your perception with that of your customers.

Recognising the total quality school

1.	Quality is outside our control	1	2	3	4	5	We are all responsible for quality
2.	The head abdicates responsibility for quality	1	2	3	4	5	The head is personally committed to quality
3.	People fit into systems	1	2	3	4	5	Systems fit people
4.	The emphasis is on detection	1	2	3	4	5	The emphasis is on prevention
5.	Values and mission are vague and assumed	1	2	3	4	5	Values and mission are explicit and lived

		1	2	3	4	5	
6.	'Training gets in the way of the real jobs'	1	2	3	4	5	'Training is the only way to improve'
7.	'There is too much change'	1	2	3	4	5	'Change is the natural process of education'
8.	'We teach pupils'	1	2	3	4	5	'We meet customer needs'
9.	'We give out information'	1	2	3	4	5	'We listen to our customers'
10.	Senior managers administer systems	1	2	3	4	5	Senior managers listen and think
11.	Mistakes are inevitable	1	2	3	4	5	Error free is the only standard
12.	Work is done by individuals	1	2	3	4	5	Work is done through teams
13.	Improving quality means more resources	1	2	3	4	5	Better does not mean more
14.	Staff have to be controlled	1	2	3	4	5	Staff must be empowered
15.	We are a good school	1	2	3	4	5	We can and must improve

The important thing about this inventory is not the actual score, although over 60 would indicate a quality management approach and below 30 should give concern, but the varying perceptions of those involved. Comparing scores will help to generate a clearer understanding of a school's present situation.

2 Defining quality

The innocent reader approaching the topic of total quality management is likely to be overwhelmed by the range of (often contradictory) advice available. The literature on quality covers the spectrum from the highly technical, mathematically inspired texts through academic discourse to the frankly anecdotal 'I did it my way – you can do it too' memoirs of captains of industry. The purpose of this chapter is to try and disentangle those elements that are most useful to managers in schools and propose a definition of TQM that is applicable to the education service.

This chapter examines the following aspects of the quality debate:

- The evolution of TQM.
- Clarification of key concepts.
- The quality 'gurus'.
- TQM in practice.
- The debate on 'excellence'.
- Quality in school management.

The evolution of TQM

Total quality management emerged in Japan in the years following the Second World War. Paradoxically the movement was inspired and sustained by two Americans, Deming and Juran. Their early work was largely concerned with statistical methods of measuring quality in the engineering industry. During the 1950s and 1960s the purely statistical approach was extended and developed by Deming and Juran and increasingly by Japanese industrialists and management writers, notably Ishikawa and Taguchi. The success of many Japanese industries in the 1960s and 1970s has been very largely credited to the quality movement. Most British homes will bear testimony to the success of the Japanese electronics industry. Virtually every British school will possess a Japanese photocopier, video player and will depend on Japanese microchips. Many British school children will watch too much TV on Japanese televisions and many sixteen year old students will aspire to own a Japanese motorbike. The lessons of quality management are already available in many schools.

It would be inappropriate and foolish to propose that what worked for Japanese industry is appropriate for British industry let alone British schools. Several writers have already pointed out that the success of Japan was due as much to national culture as to management theory. However, in the late 1970s the work of Deming in particular was 'discovered' in the USA and this led to an explosion of activity in American industry with Crosby emerging as the most influential 'evangelist'. At about the same time Peters and Waterman published *In Search of Excellence* (1982) which worked from a different set of premises but reinforced the fundamental message that explains the success of the Japanese – customer satisfaction is everything.

This message began to make an impact in Britain in the early 1980s and there have been a number of significant initiatives, notably the National Quality Campaign, the establishment of the British Quality Association in 1981 and the government White Paper *Standards, Quality and International Competitiveness* published in 1982. It is difficult, if not impossible, to quantify the impact of the quality movement on British industry, commerce and the public sector. There is evidence of increasing interest by virtue of the volume of training and consultancy taking place, the demand for BS 5750 accreditation, the job advertisements for quality managers and the number of organisations using a concept of quality in their corporate image. 1991 saw a significant awakening of interest in the education sector, notably in LEAs, higher and further education.

Clarification of key concepts

Few concepts are as open to abuse as 'quality' it is a universal panacea for organisational ills, an incontrovertible imperative and a reassuring message to clients – few will deny that they accept the value of 'quality'. The first crucial issue is to see management for quality as a process rather than a product. One of the major problems in the education service is that the achievement of quality is perceived as an intellectual problem rather than a management process. In this sense quality management becomes a search after a platonic absolute rather than an Aristotelean analysis of action to be taken. Quality has to be seen in terms of relationships rather than intangible (and unattainable) goals. To see quality as an elusive abstraction is to deny the possibility of its attainment and so justify a power based, controlling relationship. If quality is defined by providers then it will always be elusive. If it is defined by clients in terms of relationships then it becomes potentially attainable.

The status of the concept of quality largely determines the management behaviour it generates. This is best exemplified in the uncertain and often ambiguous use of the terms inspection, quality control, quality assurance and quality management. It is very important to adopt sharp definitions of these terms as the implications of each are very different. The relationship between these elements and their associated levels of management sophistication is shown in Figure 2.1.

TOTAL QUALITY MANAGEMENT	INVOLVES SUPPLIERS AND CUSTOMERS AIMING FOR CONTINUOUS IMPROVEMENT CONCERNS PRODUCTS AND PROCESSES RESPONSIBILITY WITH ALL WORKERS DELIVERED THROUGH TEAM-WORK.
QUALITY ASSURANCE	USE OF STATISTICAL PROCESS CONTROL EMPHASIS ON PREVENTION EXTERNAL ACCREDITATION DELEGATED INVOLVEMENT AUDIT OF QUALITY SYSTEMS CAUSE AND EFFECTS ANALYSIS.
QUALITY CONTROL	CONCERNED WITH PRODUCT TESTING RESPONSIBILITY WITH SUPERVISORS LIMITED QUALITY CRITERIA SOME SELF-INSPECTION PAPER BASED SYSTEMS.
INSPECTION	POST PRODUCTION REVIEW RE-WORKING REJECTION CONTROL OF WORK FORCE LIMITED TO PHYSICAL PRODUCTS.

Figure 2.1 The hierarchy of quality management (derived from Dale and Plunkett 1990, p.4)

As an organisation moves from inspection to quality management so a number of significant culture changes take place:

- there is increasing awareness and involvement of clients and suppliers;
- personal responsibility of the work force increases;
- there is increasing emphasis on process as well as product;
- the imperative is towards continuous improvement.

Fundamental to the transformation is the relationship of costs to product. Inspection might detect a 20 per cent failure rate and this might be a cause for congratulations. However, the questions remain – did the system detect all failures? Were the criteria for failure acceptable to customers? What is the impact on workers of having a fifth of the output rejected? In essence if an inspection system rejects 20 per cent then the work force are being paid to produce rubbish on one day of each week.

Most importantly inspection implies a lack of trust, an unwillingness to delegate responsibility and will inevitably create a power-dependency culture. Quality assurance goes a long way towards redressing the balance and is properly a component of TQM. It is an element of TQM and not a substitute for it. The current enthusiasm for BS 5750 is to be welcomed if it is adopted as part of an overall quality management strategy as it addresses many of the systems issues but it does not really tackle the fundamentally important process issues. Details of BS 5750 are provided in Appendix 1.

The quality 'gurus'

This section will briefly introduce the key components of the theories of the quality gurus. All are prolific in their writing and their messages are not consistent; indeed there are somewhat Byzantine ideological disputes between their adherents. The amount of contradictory advice may well induce the well known 'paralysis by analysis' syndrome. It is not proposed to offer systematic comparative review but rather highlight the key components of each writer's thinking.

Crosby

Crosby is probably the most significant writer in terms of influence in the USA and Europe. He focuses on senior management and argues the centrality of increased profitability through quality improvement. He is best known for his four absolutes of quality management:

1. The definition   Quality is conformance to customer
                    requirements, not intrinsic goodness.
2. The system   Prevention, not detection.
3. The standard   Zero defects.
4. The measurement The price of non-conformance.

These absolutes have been adopted by many companies and have
almost become synonymous with TQM. Their relevance to schools
will be discussed below but it would be wrong to pretend that they
are unproblematic in any context. In particular it is argued that zero
defects as a performance standard is hopelessly unrealistic. However, the conceptual framework the absolutes offer do help to
distinguish TQM from other management approaches. Equally
useful are Crosby's fourteen steps to quality improvement – the basis
for implementation in many companies.

Crosby's fourteen steps

1. Establish full management commitment to the quality
   programme.
2. Set up a quality team to drive the programme.
3. Introduce quality measurement procedures.
4. Define and apply the principle of the cost of quality.
5. Institute a quality awareness programme.
6. Introduce corrective action procedures.
7. Plan for the implementation of zero defects.
8. Implement supervisor training.
9. Announce zero defects day to launch the process.
10. Set goals to bring about action.
11. Set up employee–management communications systems.
12. Recognise those who have actively participated.
13. Set up quality councils to sustain the process.
14. Do it all over again.

These steps have been criticised as being too doctrinaire and not
always appropriate to different company cultures.

Deming

Deming's approach to quality management is derived from statistical
methodologies. Deming advocates the use of statistical methods to
reduce variability and so improve production. He argues that 85 per
cent of production faults are the responsibility of management – not
employees. Inspection is inappropriate because it is post-facto,

usually ineffective and costly. Instead he proposes an emphasis on precision, performance and attention to customers' requirements; for Deming this is best done through statistical methods designed to reduce variation. Like Crosby, Deming has synthesized his views on quality management into 14 points:

Deming's fourteen points for management

1. Create constancy of purpose for continual improvement of products and services.
2. Adopt the new philosophy and abandon traditional ways of working.
3. Move from inspection to building quality into every product and process.
4. Stop awarding contracts on the basis of lowest bid – specify and buy quality.
5. Engage in a process of continually improving every aspect of company activity.
6. Use work based training techniques.
7. The emphasis for leaders and managers must be on quality, not quantity.
8. Drive out fear by improving communication.
9. Break down organisation barriers.
10. Eliminate slogans and exhortations.
11. Eliminate arbitrary numerical targets.
12. Allow for pride of workmanship by locating responsibility with the worker.
13. Encourage education and self-development.
14. Create a management structure and culture that will drive the preceding 13 points.

Deming has been criticised for the perceived banality of these points. However, his philosophy has been widely adopted and applied and it is highly congruent with other theorists.

Juran

Joseph Juran is generally recognised as the most intellectually profound of the management theorists. Juran defines quality as 'fitness for purpose' and identifies the principal outcome of quality management as reducing the cost of quality and increasing conformance. He identifies three steps to quality improvement:

1. Structural annual improvement plans.
2. Training for the whole organisation.

3.   Quality directed leadership.

Juran identifies the following components of a systematic approach to a company-wide quality programme:

1.   Identify goals and policies for quality.
2.   Implement plans to meet the goals.
3.   Provide resources to evaluate progress.
4.   Ensure appropriate motivation.

As with the other 'gurus' Juran has summarised his principles of quality management into a series of epithets.

Juran's ten steps to quality improvement

1.   Create awareness of the need and opportunity for improvement.
2.   Set explicit goals for improvement.
3.   Create an organisational structure to drive the improvement process.
4.   Provide appropriate training.
5.   Adopt a project approach to problem solving.
6.   Identify and report progress.
7.   Recognise and reinforce success.
8.   Communicate results.
9.   Keep records of changes.
10. Build an annual improvement cycle into all company processes.

Juran places great emphasis on leadership and team-work arguing that quality management is a balance of human relations skills and statistical process control skills.

Crosby, Deming and Juran may be safely credited with creating the vocabulary of total quality management although there are significant differences between them. There are a substantial number of other theorists and a rapidly increasing number of commentators. Feigenbaum is noteworthy in that he is generally credited with linking 'total' and 'quality'. Feigenbaum's approach is technical and highly detailed but he does stress the importance of quality approaches permeating every aspect of an organisation. Conway stresses the importance of total quality management as a process rather than an objective – he proposes six basic tools for quality improvement:

- human relations skills;
- statistical data collection;
- use of statistical display techniques to inform;
- statistical process control, measuring to reduce variation;
- imagineering – visualising an ideal state;
- organising work to facilitate improvement.

The Japanese influence on the west has been limited but is now increasing particularly in the areas of implementation and the development of analytical techniques. The most significant contributors in this field are Ishikawa and Taguchi.

Although it is easy to parody the differences between the gurus and become very depressed at the sheer volume of advice and exhortation, all the writers are practical exponents of their theories and they have made their theories work.

TQM in practice

It is not the purpose of this section to identify TQM companies and then exhort schools to do likewise – quite the reverse. The following examples are offered to demonstrate the practical realities of adopting a quality approach and to demonstrate a crucial fact – that there are no 'off-the-shelf' solutions to the issue of quality.

Marks and Spencer

Perversely Marks and Spencer is not a TQM company, it has not followed or adopted the teachings of any of the American gurus. There is a very strong case for arguing that Sieff (1991) should be included in the pantheon of the quality 'greats'. In many ways Marks and Spencer have been practising TQM for over half a century, and the company name is synonymous with quality in British retailing.

The company's image, status and success are founded on the simple principle of pleasing the customer by getting quality right first and then dealing with issues of price and returns. The company's motivation is primarily a moral one and this influences every facet of corporate culture and operating procedures. A number of very specific strategies can be identified:

- Customer orientation: This applies to product range, price and quality *and* to personal relationships, responses to complaints, the notion of customer entitlement and continual responsiveness.
- Personnel issues: Marks and Spencer is famous for its

treatment of its staff, they are treated with trust and respect and work in a quality environment in terms of welfare, employment conditions and development.

- Suppliers: The company has long operated a quality relationship with its suppliers which works in two ways. Firstly Marks and Spencer are involved in every aspect of the production process; standards are published for raw materials and manufacturing processes; there is a certification process for suppliers and technical support to develop new products. Secondly there are explicit expectations as to the nature of the relationship between supplier and customer.
- Codifying procedures: All procedures are standardised and documented for both internal operations and for suppliers. Operational simplicity is a driving force.
- Bench marking: The company is constantly and acutely aware of the performance of competitors; analysing rival products and identifying areas for development. This process is reflected in the work of the technical departments which analyse every aspect of a product.

Perhaps the most significant feature of Marks and Spencer is the acute and company wide awareness of the need to constantly focus on quality. No organisation could possibly hope to replicate the Marks and Spencer approach by a process of duplication. With Marks and Spencer quality is not a 'what' or a 'how' but a 'why' – it is the *raison d'etre* of the company.

The National Trust

Webb (1991) argues that the National Trust is a classic example of how a service, i.e. non-profit organisation, can work towards quality. Webb argues that the criteria for quality in a service organisation are derived from the organisation's objectives, how well they are met and whether or not they conform with quality (p.83). He argues that the NT meets its objectives in that it maximises access and conservation, increases its preservation work whilst respecting the interests of a wide range of pressure groups.

The factors which lead to this perceived quality are, according to Webb:

- clarity and consistency of philosophy and strategy;
- clear decision-making structures;
- decentralised staff with a high degree of specialisation;
- clarity of communication channels;

- objective budgeting;
- clear delineations of policy making, management and specialist functions;
- high motivation of full-time staff and volunteers.

Although the trust is a unique organisation and it is difficult to
extrapolate from it to the education service the related notions of
clarity of purpose, relevant structure and effective communications
are valid.

Harvard University

The Office for Information Technology (OIT) at Harvard University
has introduced TQM defining quality as 'the alignment of all the
processes in an organisation to assure full customer satisfaction'. The
Harvard Quality Programme (HQP) shapes the way in which OIT
operates, it is centrally focused on customer satisfaction. Customers
are anyone, external or internal, who seeks a product or service. The
major components of HQP are:

- team-work and participation of all staff;
- leadership committed to excellence;
- strategic planning;
- skill building for all staff;
- continuous improvement of work processes;
- co-operation between departments.

In essence HQP has changed the culture of OIT from problem
solving and decision making by individuals in a style that excludes
others to problem solving using teams and a common approach.

Although OIT operates in a commercial environment in that it has to
compete for university business it does provide a possible model for the
application of TQM in an essentially service orientated, educational
environment. **(Derived from Harvard University Staff Newspaper)**

ICI

Every visitor to an ICI works is presented with a card outlining
safety procedures; on one side of the card is the simple message
'Safety first, quality second, profits third'. This exemplifies the
philosophy of one of Britain's most consistently successful industrial
concerns. The reasons for this success have been the subject of much
debate and analysis, but Lessem (1985) advances the following
reasons:

1 A belief in the importance of the individual and that the organisation must be built around the individual.
2. An emphasis on the importance of corporate renewal constantly growing and evolving.
3. Integration of business, technological and personal development.
4. Leadership concerned with vision and enabling.
5. Creation of an open, collaborative culture.
6. An obsession with technical excellence, 'delighting the customer' with better quality, better value and innovative products.

Much has been made of the inspirational leadership of ICI by John Harvey Jones, although he would minimise his personal impact. There is no doubt that quality companies have changed and developed through visionary leadership rather than dutiful role following.

It was not the intention of this section to offer paragons of virtue to be emulated, but rather to stress the importance of any organisation having a view of what it wants to be and how to achieve that vision. Crucial to the examples cited is the detailed extrapolation from principle into practice and, crucially, the importance of consistency in *all* processes. There are doubtless many schools and colleges which could legitimately claim inclusion in any listing of organisations driven by quality principles but the evidence is yet to be collected and codified.

The debate on 'excellence'

The excellence movement parallels the rise of total quality management in that both were initiated in the USA in the late 1970s. In 1980 Hayes and Abernathy published an article in the *Harvard Business Review* 'Managing our way to economic decline'. The article was a searing indictment of the prevailing management orthodoxy in the United States. They argued that the emergence of Japan as an economic superpower was primarily due to a failure of management rather than new factories and cheap labour in the far east or problems with unions and government at home. The real problem was a lack of vision and leadership, American managers were preoccupied with a short-term financial approach to managing industry and commerce.

Peters and Waterman

In 1982 Peters and Waterman published *In Search of Excellence* which has now sold five million copies world-wide. It built on the hypothesis advanced by Hayes and Abernathy and is generally credited with changing the prevailing management culture in the west. The book is essentially an analysis of what were generally recognised as successful companies. On the basis of this analysis Peters and Waterman extrapolated the essential characteristics for success:

- A bias for action
- Close to the customer.
- Autonomy.
- Productivity through people.
- Hands on, value driven management.
- Stick to the knitting.
- Simple forms, lean staff.
- Simultaneous loose-tight properties.

In a subsequent work with Austin *A Passion for Excellence* Peters reduced the eight points to three fundamental factors: care of customers, innovation and concern for people linked by what Peters calls 'management by walking about' (MBWA), i.e. proactive leadership.

The work of Peters and Waterman inspired parallel studies in a number of western countries; in Britain Goldsmith and Clutterbuck published *The Winning Streak* in 1984. Their study paralleled *In Search of Excellence* in a number of important respects:

- Visible top management with clear objectives.
- Autonomy for natural work units.
- Balancing tight control with areas for flexibility.
- High levels of commitment and involvement.
- Emphasis on customer satisfaction.
- Sticking to the basic principles of the business.
- Commitment to innovation and change.
- Integrity in all dealings.

There were substantial criticisms of the 'excellence approach', a number of the companies cited ran into severe difficulties almost immediately following publication and the research methodology was criticised as superficial and anecdotal. However, the impact of the movement cannot be denied if only for changing the language of management.

Peters has recognised the problems and the changing environment in his most recent work *Thriving on Chaos*. Rather than trying to establish immutable principles, Peters now argues for organisational uniqueness with a highly responsive management style and structure based on:

- obsessional responsiveness to customers;
- constant innovation;
- empowering individuals;
- leadership based on an inspiring vision;
- the introduction of simple quantifiable control systems.

The parallels with the precepts of the TQM gurus are clear and serve to reinforce the view that there may be a minimalist view as to the principles informing quality management.

Kanter

Rosabeth Moss Kanter is regarded as one of the most intellectually and academically robust of the writers on excellence. Her books *The Change Masters* and *When Giants Learn to Dance* provide a sophisticated analysis of the social and organisational issues influencing corporate success or failure. As with Peters her preoccupation is with change and it is almost possible to reduce her writing to the simple hypothesis that excellence = the capacity to change. She argues that a change culture has the following characteristics:

- It encourages people to be enterprising, to solve problems by operating organisational systems, practices and rewards that reinforce and encourage innovative behaviour.
- It is based on small teams, teams which have autonomy and are able to complete a specified taste.
- It has a 'culture of pride' which respects individual creativity and problem solving and denies mediocrity and inferiority.

Her more detailed prescriptions (again the almost mystical points) include references to participation, choice, openness, commitment, explicit standards, rewarding success and creating excitement.

Quality in school management

The purpose of this section is to integrate what has been examined so far in this chapter and to propose a model for total quality management in schools. It is not intended to propose a blueprint. As has already been stressed each organisation must develop its own approach. What follows are a series of proposals to help in the analysis of existing management strategies and serve as the basis for the formulation of a strategy. This chapter has very briefly highlighted the components of the major theories and illustrations of TQM in practice – obviously not all of what has been described is relevant to schools.

The concept of 'right first time' is obviously highly problematic in an educational context when there is effectively no control over the intake into the school system. However, 'right first time' applies to processes as well as products and therefore has relevance. Equally the elaborate details of statistical process control are clearly relevant to complex engineering processes but less so to a primary school reception class or the counselling system in a large comprehensive. However, there is much that can be accepted and applied. Much of what is proposed already exists in the literature of school management – however, it has not been integrated into a coherent and comprehensive whole.

Even the most superficial reading of the literature on quality and excellence allows the identifications of a number of key features:

1. Quality is defined by the customer, not the supplier.
2. Quality consists of meeting stated needs, requirements and standards.
3. Quality is achieved through continuous improvement, by prevention, not detection.
4. Quality is driven by senior management but is an equal responsibility of all those involved in any process.
5. Quality is measured by statistical methods, the 'cost of quality' is the cost of non-conformance. Communicate with facts.
6. Quality has to pervade human relationships in the work place, teams are the most powerful agent for managing quality.
7. Quality can only be achieved by a valued work force; education, training and personal growth are essential to this.
8. Quality has to be the criterion for reviewing every decision, every action and every process.

Summary

– Total quality management is increasingly the norm in industrial and commercial organisations.
– Quality management is a specific term that has to be distinguished from quality control and quality assurance.
– There is a voluminous literature on quality and excellence but

the key issues can be distilled into a few precepts.
- Adopting TQM is an explanation of the dominance of a number of well known organisations.
- It is possible to isolate a number of features of TQM theory that are not specific to the commercial sector.

Action

- If you use the word quality in your school's aims what *exactly* do you mean?
- Have you identified your school's clients? Is your view shared by all your colleagues?
- Is your senior management team really a team or just a meeting?
- Does your school prepare its pupils for work in a TQM company?
- How well do you communicate as a manager? How do you know?
- If you reject the experience of industry and commerce do you have an equally systematic alternative?
- If schools are not about managing quality then what are they about?

3   Customer satisfaction

The quality organisation exists for its customers, it has no other purpose other than providing products and services which satisfy customer needs. The commercial organisation which fails to meet its customers' requirements will rapidly go out of business. The rest of this book is devoted to principles and processes to help ensure a focus on the customer. This chapter is concerned with explaining the issues involved in the concept of customer. There are many problems associated with using the term 'customer' in an educational context; there is no cash transaction, education is a statutory requirement, in many parts of the country there is no choice of school available so the notion of customer choice is spurious. More significant is the objection that education is a professional relationship so the term 'client' is more appropriate and the role of schools is not to perpetuate existing social norms but rather to enhance society, to pass on moral, intellectual and social skills to children.

This view presupposes a unique body of knowledge to which access is restricted, teachers are the custodians of that knowledge and transmit it according to best professional practice. The customer can't know best because the customer doesn't know. A quality approach denies the validity of this approach. The 1988 Education Reform Act has done much to challenge this view by giving parents the potential power to choose. Many trends in schools have highlighted the issue of responsiveness to children, community and the full range of stake-holders in education.

The purpose of this chapter is to examine the components of customer satisfaction through a variety of issues:

- Defining the customer.
- The nature of quality customer service.
- Ensuring customer satisfaction.

Defining the customer

Figure 3.1A caricatures the traditional customer relationship in education – passive recipients of a professional service rather like patients in a hospital bed being talked about rather than listened to. It is easy to parody this situation – 'no parents past this point'; 'generally satisfactory work and progress'; the options booklet that assumes training in deductive logic; the school prospectus written by teachers for teachers; the exclusion of non-teachers from the staff room; home work instructions so cryptic that the allocated time is spent deciphering them. These are all minor irritants or symptomatic of a failure to perceive customer needs and expectations.

The academic debate about who is the customer in education is capable of metaphysical convolutions; working on permutations of professionality, professionalism, accountability, answerability a wide range of answers are possible. The TQM response is quite simple and central to this book:

> A CUSTOMER IS ANYONE TO WHOM
> A PRODUCT OR SERVICE IS PROVIDED.

A customer is therefore defined in terms of relationships and processes rather than relative status, role or function. Customers are internal and external. The quality approach to customers is shown in Figure 3.1B.

The implications of this model are:

- Everyone is a supplier and a customer.
- There are equal responsibilities on suppliers and customers.
- Work processes have to be defined in terms of customers and suppliers.
- It may be helpful to differentiate between internal and external customers and suppliers but not to discriminate in levels of service.
- Supplier–customer 'chains' may be of variable length but this cannot be used as an excuse to compromise the process.

In order to ensure the integrity of the chain a significant amount

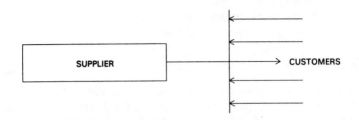

A.   The Traditional Supplier - Customer Relationship

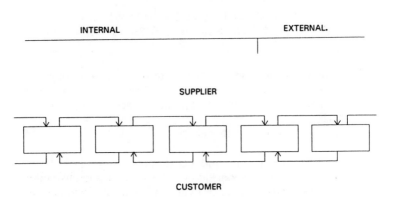

B.   Quality Supplier - Customer Relationships

Figure 3.1   Supplier–customer relationships

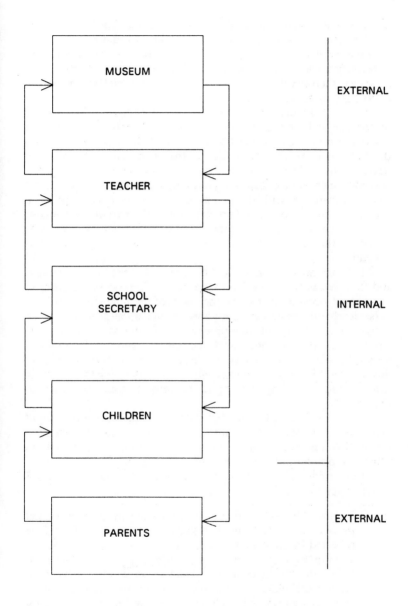

Figure 3.2   Supplier–customer relationships in organising a class trip

of analysis is required to establish who exactly is involved – unless this first step is taken then quality will be problematic.

Figure 3.2 shows the supplier–customer relationship involved in organising a class trip to a museum. Unless all the participants are identified then it will be impossible to identify requirements and so impossible to provide quality service.

If one component is missed then the information flow will be incomplete and the trip will probably not take place. There may be associated processes, the teacher liaising with the head teacher, with the bus company etc. Each link in the chain has to be of equal strength; the information from the museum has to be complete–opening times, eating facilities, educational support services, prices etc. However, this will be to no avail if the letter is not typed and copied in time, if children do not deliver it and if parents do not have a date by which to return it. At each stage requirements have to be stated so that customers and suppliers are aware of their inter-dependence.

In this example parents might be regarded as the 'final' customer and their needs therefore determine the whole process. In order to make the process a quality one the needs of the final customer have to be clearly understood and expressed in such a way as to inform the design and delivery of the process. This involves defining the customer and then developing mechanisms to ensure monitoring and feedback. These mechanisms are discussed in the third section of this chapter, 'Ensuring customer satisfaction'; defining the customer involves understanding a complex range of factors, as shown in Figure 3.3.

Many schools could argue that they have a full understanding of their customers. However, care has to be taken in the extent to which this understanding is imposed by teachers, is based on subjective opinion or swayed by political opinion.

The components of defining the customer outlined in Figure 3.3 may be expanded as follows:

- Values: This is the significance attached to the educational process in general and the school in particular. It will be reflected in the extent to which education is seen by parents as an investment or an expedient, the importance attached to the school by the community and the credibility it has with other stakeholders. Unless the school understands the values of its customers it is unlikely to be able to deliver quality outcomes.
- Attitudes: In some senses attitudes might be regarded as the manifestation of values – responses to the school displayed in

In order to understand your customers you need information about their:

Values :

Attitudes :

Educational Level :

Expectations :

Preferences :

Social Situation :

Commitment :

Figure 3.3 Defining the customer

behaviour. Attitudes are reflected in the language, involvement and commitment of the school's customers. The school that aspires to provide a quality service to its customers looks to itself first as the cause of behaviour on the part of its clients. Attitudes change and develop in response to the service provided.

– Educational level: Most professionals are so immersed in their expertise that it is possible to forget that the rest of the community does not necessarily share their understanding. Just as teachers are sometimes confused by medical or legal language so their clients can be intimidated by inappropriate language.

No effective teacher would ever dream of teaching a lesson without checking that the vocabulary was appropriate and the concepts understood. The same principle applies to all those with whom the school communicates. This is not to argue for simplification to the point of absurdity but rather effective communication.

- Expectations: Meeting customer expectations is the hall mark of quality – exceeding them is the key characteristic of total quality. However, this means that they have to be known and understood. Expectations are more than requirements – they are the basis of 'delighting the customer'. It is easy for a garage or shop to exceed customer expectations, less so for a school to ensure that every child is happy and fulfilled, achieves at least 5 GCSE passes or gets a job. Yet one of the principal features of successful schools is that they share and express high expectations.

- Preferences: All organisations that provide a service will usually offer a range of options in order to maximise the possibilities of anticipating customer choice. Understanding the broad preferences of customers is a fundamental component of providing a quality service. The details are to be negotiated and developed on the basis of feedback but the broad pattern of preferences has to be established; this might include issues such as uniform, the pattern of the school day, sex education, religious education etc.

- Social situation: The social context of a school will be a major determinant of its response to many of its customers. Prevailing patterns of culture, the ethnic balance, unemployment, the economic situation, social advantage and deprivation will all be significant features in helping to determine a school's response to its community. Schools are often highly expert in understanding the context in which they operate. The difference for a TQM school is the extent to which responses are assumed and derived by teachers or based on real understanding.

- Commitment: Commercial success depends on obtaining and retaining customers. Increasingly schools are in the same situation – failure to recruit and retain pupils will result in the school ceasing to be viable. It is therefore essential to understand the significance attached to education by customers, in order to be able to make the most appropriate responses. Figure 3.4 shows one way of understanding the implications of varying levels of commitment.
For a relatively prosperous community the relative levels of significance and commitment might appear as shown, however, the situation could be totally reversed in other communities. The commitment of parents will be a direct function of the significance attached to education and this will in turn reflect the six components identified above.

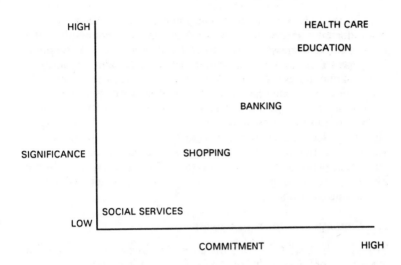

Figure 3.4 Understanding the relationship between significance and commitment

Defining the customer is essential with regard to parents and children and they should be the predominant feature of any such analysis. However, the same process is needed for all customers especially the external ones. There is a potential issue in that perceptions and needs may be in conflict – different groups may have varying expectations. This issue is best resolved by analysis of the particular process and identifying the 'end user' who is then the customer whose needs predominate. This does not mean that managing a quality school is simply a series of conditioned responses. There is an imperative to enhance the service provided, to 'delight the customer' and most importantly to add value. TQM organisations are successful because they build on customer expectations and continually enhance the service provided. However the starting point must be the values, attitudes, educational level, expectations, preferences, social situations and commitment of customers.

The nature of quality customer service

This is the aspect of quality management that it is most easy to misunderstand and misapply. Customer service is not about potted plants, carpets, glossy brochures and carefully scripted receptionists. These factors can be significant but are only manifestations of a fundamental obsession with satisfying the customer. There is a temptation to assume that smartness equals quality but there is little point in having a sophisticated reception area if it is difficult to find, if the appropriate person is not available and if the quality of children's learning is not the central focus of any discussion. Reviews of the literature on customer service produce lists of strategies, many of which fall into the 'have a nice day' syndrome. However, it is possible to isolate a range of factors which are appropriate to schools.

1. Conformance to requirements

This is at the heart of quality management. In essence it means that the service provided is fit for the purpose intended, i.e. it meets the needs of the customer. There are many potential applications of this principle in schools:

- reporting on progress to parents; the information is expressed in such a way as to be comprehensible and comprehensive;
- purchase of text books; they are relevant, up-to-date, written at an appropriate level with a suitable format;
- classroom organisation; facilities and resources are easily available.

This list could be continued indefinitely and it is an important part of the implementation process to find out and deliver these needs. However, the most important potential application is in the organisation of learning. Conformance to requirements does raise significant questions about the delivery of the curriculum. If the needs of the individual learner are considered the starting point for identifying customer needs then a number of issues emerge:

- the need to relate learning strategies to individual ability;
- the flexible use of time to allow appropriate pacing and completion of integrated units of study;
- deployment of the full range of teaching strategies from the most didactic to the most flexible – to be determined by need not ideology;

- reviewing the role of the teacher as controller and emphasising the role of facilitator;
- questioning teaching the 'class' when individual outcomes are the determinants of educational success;
- recognition of the importance of intellectual and social skills development being reflected in the organisation of learning;
- ensuring that marking and assessment are formative rather than summative;
- programming options to ensure that individual rather than systems needs are met.

This approach would appear to endorse an open or flexible learning approach and this would appear to be the strategy that is closest to quality principles. However, a quality approach to managing learning is not a matter of prescribing the 'one best way' but rather diagnosing and identifying needs and relating learning strategies to them. What the quality approach does question is the view of managing learning for administrative convenience. As has been mentioned elsewhere in this book the effective primary classroom is probably the closest that education currently comes to TQM.

2. Continuous improvement

In terms of customer satisfaction continuous improvement means that suppliers are constantly concerned with adding value. There is an obsession with enhancing and improving every process. This is where professional expertise and development are so important. It is the professional skills and knowledge of teachers and managers in schools that are the principal source of this process. At the most fundamental level it is how the teaching of a particular topic can be improved the next time it is taught, how teaching aids and resources can be deployed to better effect.

This is a natural process for professionals – never accepting the 'status-quo' but constantly explaining techniques to ensure more complete understanding, to improve the language used in materials, to develop activities that help clarify complex issues.

The same principles apply to management processes in schools, induction procedures, decision making, INSET days are all capable of sustained improvement over time. The crucial thing is that there is no complacency, no notion of a plateau of acceptability.

3. Responsiveness

This is one of the most tangible expressions of a customer

satisfaction orientation. In practical terms it means a rapid response to complaints and requests. More directly the phone is answered promptly, letters are replied to within a specified time period; more importantly there is a tangible and personal response on the customers' terms. This might mean an 'open door' policy. It certainly means that concerns are given a high degree of seriousness.

In the classroom it means creating the situation where children feel able, and are encouraged to express concerns which are dealt with. It also means that ideas and suggestions are incorporated rapidly in order to improve classroom and school processes.

4. Integration

Customers are fully integrated into the organisation. This means that possible customer response is the baseline criterion in every decision making process and that customers are physically incorporated into activities. It is better to involve at the outset than to decide, consult and then have to change.

This is much more than encouraging a PTA, holding parents' evenings or inviting parents in to help. It is actively, deliberately and systematically informing and involving all customers in processes. Low levels of interest are usually explained by low levels of perceived significance. Genuine integration means that customers will be able to see tangible outcomes of their involvement rather than a token acknowledgement.

In practical terms this means maximum contact at appropriate levels; in the secondary school making the form tutor the first point of contact with parents; the notion of the 'open day' needs to be replaced by the concept of permanent openness. The non-teaching staff of the school need to be fully incorporated into all aspects of the quality strategy. Crucially administrative systems and structures should not be used as barriers to incorporation and involvement. Secondary and primary school staff need to visit and exchange as do secondary and college staff. The National Curriculum requires partnership through integration if it is to work for the benefit of children. Many schools have found that the best way to deal with bullying, theft, vandalism etc. is not to make more rules but to hand the problem, its solution and implementation to children.

This is a classic example of real integration and it is much more likely to succeed because it takes into account the views of those involved and also has their commitment. This is listening to the customer and demonstrating tangible respect.

5. Focus on delivery

The quality organisation centres all its resources on those who are in direct contact with the customer. In the case of schools this is obviously the classroom teacher. The focus for concern, support and development has to be those who actually deliver. Their development has to be the central priority and the way in which the school is managed has to reflect the importance of the classroom teacher. They are the management team's most important internal customer.

The best word to describe the relationship between management team and teacher is probably *respect*, i.e. recognition of the central significance of the classroom practitioner.

One of the best ways of ensuring customer satisfaction is to ensure that those with whom customers come into contact have the skills to be able to respond and confide in senior management. This requires support praise, recognition, thanks and trust. In practical terms this means direct and immediate support for teachers in the classroom, budgeting so as to maximise resources at the focal point of the school and the provision of quality INSET to meet classroom needs.

A further manifestation of this is the involvement of senior management by being directly available to classroom teachers and by being involved in the classroom and other aspects of the school on a regular basis. This can take a wide variety of forms, e.g. covering for absence, having a programme of regular cover to create opportunities for feedback – and time for colleagues, taking teachers off timetables for a week to allow time for projects etc.

The crucial thing is that managers do not 'lose touch' and are directly available to improve responsiveness. Much is made in the literature of the quality movement of management by walking about (MBWA). Better than this is MBDTJ – managing by doing the job. This is not to diminish the strategic role of senior management but to stress the importance of keeping close to the customer and seeing the school through its customers' eyes.

6. Listening to the customer

Quality customer service can only be achieved through real listening; such is the importance of this topic that it is the subject of the third section of this chapter. Delivering quality customer service is a matter of respecting the uniqueness of each customer, treating them with respect and listening to them.

Ensuring customer satisfaction

Measuring customer satisfaction is at the heart of TQM – obtaining feedback and *acting on it* is what differentiates TQM from every other management theory. There is a moral obligation on all suppliers to find out customer needs, to seek to meet them and then to find out the extent to which they have been met. There is an equal obligation on customers to articulate requirements and then to participate in monitoring and review. This section is concerned with some of the methods available to gather data, many of these are familiar to most schools – the crucial difference is the extent to which listening takes place and action results.

The following techniques are among the most appropriate for schools:

1. Suggestion cards

Invite all the school's customers, internal and external, to suggest improvements. The natural creativity of children can be a powerful force as can parents after two hours spent in school for a total of 20 minutes' consultation with teachers. The only rule is to offer solutions as well as identifying problems. This approach can also be used to solve a particular problem. The important thing is that the cards are seen to lead to action and not used as a spurious form of PR.

2. Shadowing

Suppliers place themselves in the situation of customers. A form teacher in a secondary school spends the day with her form (and is not allowed in the staff room at break or lunch-time!). A primary teacher joins his former pupils on their first day in secondary school, a secondary school timetabler experiences the fruits of her labours by experiencing the reality of the pro-graph board! Senior staff teach the problem class.

Although the shadow's presence will inevitably distort 'reality' the process does provide the opportunity for experiencing the direct impact of school policies.

3. Interviews

These can be used with almost any group as the basis for detailed and informed data collection. Talking to small groups of children, inviting representatives of the local community, groups of governors and teachers to indicate how the school might be improved are all

potentially powerful strategies to generate ideas, to indicate seriousness and demonstrate commitment.

4. Surveys

These are probably the most powerful, and potentially most
intimidating means of obtaining feedback. They are important
because they are capable of quantification and will thus permit
comparisons over time. Quantification also facilitates prioritisation.
Surveys can be used to:

- collect information about customer needs;
- identify specific problems;
- assess conformity to requirements;
- measure satisfaction.

Thus surveys may be used about a specific lesson, a particular aspect
of school life, meetings, evaluation of a course of study, a specific
facility (e.g. the library) or views on a current issue (e.g. uniform).

The design of the survey should be determined by the data
required but may include:

- open-ended questions; a useful source of data but difficult to
  analyse;
- closed questions; easy to analyse but limited options);
- rating scales; easy to complete and analyse but requiring
  careful design.

The data that is collected can be analysed using a variety of
techniques such as Pareto Analysis. The results of a survey can
provide:

- instant feedback;
- diagnosis of specific problem areas;
- indications of satisfaction and success;
- decisions about priorities for action;
- evidence of commitment to customer satisfaction.

5. Team meetings

Almost any team can contribute to feedback by having a regular
agenda item concerned with feedback to suppliers. It may be
appropriate to constitute teams for the specific purpose of reviewing
services provided. A team may also invite some of its customers to
attend its meetings on a regular basis. Aspects of some lessons, e.g.

personal and social education can be devoted to the provision of feedback. This survey is potentially one of the most powerful as it integrates review and feedback into normal operating processes. As confidence grows within a team so feedback will become more detailed and specific.

Although review and monitoring are essential they are symptomatic of a school which is listening to its customers and trying to see itself through their eyes. If the customer chain is fully established then there will be a gradual shift from reaction to anticipation and the school's customers will be fully integrated into all aspects of its working processes. The full involvement of children in this process can be viewed as an important, and living, contribution to their preparation for adulthood by learning how to participate in a wide range of social processes – not least their own obligations as suppliers of products and services. Seeing children as customers in the classroom and school processes also minimises the view that management approaches turn them into products.

Summary

- Quality organisations exist to meet customer needs.
- A customer is anyone to whom a product or service is provided.
- There are internal and external customers.
- It is the responsibility of customers to specify needs and suppliers to meet them.
- Customers need to be defined in terms of a complex range of factors.
- Customer needs are defined in specific actions.
- Customers must be listened to – complaints and concerns must be welcomed.
- A range of techniques can be used to find out about customer satisfaction.
- Children are not products – they are customers.

Action

- Identify your customers and find out their requirements.
- Analyse areas of strength and weakness.
- Build review procedures into every process.
- Create a climate for delighting the customer.

4 Managing quality processes

Quality organisations are obsessed with measurement. Every aspect of every process is measured and one of the first signs of trusting the work force is to delegate the responsibility for statistical processes to operative level. Measurement is used to ensure conformity to standards, to identify the cost of deviation and to monitor the impact of improvements. Very limited changes in vocabulary are necessary to find parallels in schools – the use of registers, marking and assessment, reading ages and setting are all forms of quantification used in the management of children's learning. This chapter argues that a similar approach is necessary in the management of all school processes. Three main issues are discussed.

- understanding process in schools;
- the cost of quality;
- techniques for improving work processes.

The key purpose of improving work processes is to add value, to make the process and thereby its product closer to customer requirements and so of higher quality. Adding value is a matter of listening to customers and making modifications in the light of their feedback. Each improvement, each development makes it more likely that the product or process will conform to customer expectations and so retain their loyalty. Adding value is not a matter of embellishment or increasing complexity but getting ever closer to customer specification. In schools, for example, this does not necessarily mean more resources, it means meetings that solve problems, lessons that are understood, INSET days that can be applied in practical terms.

Understanding processes in schools

Educational processes are extraordinarily complex given the enormous variability of inputs, the interactions that take place and the often ambiguous outcomes. If education is perceived as a life long process with most of the factors outside the control of schools then it could be argued that it is impossible to analyse the process. However, this is to deny or minimise the reality of school life which is made up of concrete activities most of which are planned and structured and for which the inputs are carefully calculated and deployed. Although classroom processes are complex, and properly the subject of another book, management processes in schools are appropriate for analysis. The objective of all management processes is to meet the requirements of the customer; 'problems' in the management of schools are almost invariably due to a failure in a process which can be analysed and corrected. In its simplest form, a work process has the components shown in Figure 4.1.

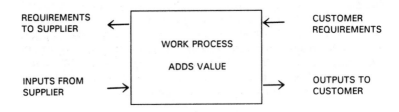

Figure 4.1   Work processes

The work process is thus the link in the customer–supplier chain and it requires:

- articulation and communication of customer requirements;
- articulation and communication of requirements of the supplier;
- the provision of the skills, resources and procedures necessary to complete the process.

If this third element is added then the process model becomes much more detailed, as shown in Figure 4.2.

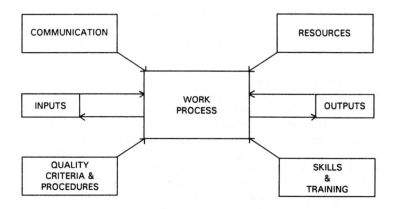

Figure 4.2 The components of work processes

In order for the process to work all the aspects identified have to be complete; lack of definition in any respect will compromise the potential to meet customer requirements. A simple example – a letter to parents about a trip illustrates the point.

- The supplier is the teacher planning the trip. The requirements on her are to supply the school secretary with all the necessary data in a legible form.
- The customer is a parent whose requirements include; all the relevant data expressed in a clear format in plenty of time and a clear indication of what action is required.
- The process is managed by the secretary who needs time to complete the task, access to the word processor and photocopier, school guide-lines on the format of the letter, procedures for distribution, the time to check the letter with the teacher. This all assumes skills with the word processor and photocopier which should not be taken for granted.

All of these elements are necessary if there is to be a quality product. Although this example may be trivial the implications of not managing the process are substantial:

- Time is wasted by teacher and secretary in checking, clarifying or correcting.
- Re-working the letter would double the cost in terms of time, paper and copying.

- If the letter is sent out incomplete then time would be wasted in answering queries.
- Incorrect information might result in a limited response so causing the trip to be cancelled.

The financial cost of reissuing such a letter might be £50 (£12 for teacher time, £8 secretarial time, £5 copying × 2) and this is avoidable waste. Few teachers would throw away £25 worth of stock but many will lose much more in wasted time because of a failure to prevent errors. This direct waste is, at least, matched by the frustration, loss of credibility, opportunity cost and poor reputation for efficiency arising from such an incident.

It is comparatively easy to assign a cash value to a range of examples: a senior management team meeting that fails to reach a solution to a problem and has to reconvene could be costed at £100; the social cost is significantly higher. A primary school staff meeting where a circular is read to the staff for 30 minutes probably costs £40 in terms of salary but far more in resentment and a sense of powerlessness.

In order to ensure the optimum use of resources the emphasis in managing has to be on prevention – one of the cornerstones of TQM. In the example described above the costs resulting from an incorrect letter were discovered by inspection, i.e. after the event and therefore had to be corrected; the additional costs arose from inspection and could have been negated by a policy of prevention, i.e. finding out needs and working to established procedures. Prevention has to be built into working procedures through a variety of techniques. This is where BS 5750 is of particular importance and help (see Appendix 1).

Prevention in an industrial context is very much concerned with establishing a range of highly detailed statistical process control techniques. It is difficult, if not impossible to translate these into an educational environment. However, there is a model in the use of testing in the classroom – if that test is used to modify teaching strategies rather than simply recorded, and used as a measure of ignorance rather than as feedback on teaching methods. Some possible applications of these techniques to management processes are outlined in section 3 of this chapter.

Prevention is directly linked to knowledge; it is a central responsibility of management to ensure that requirements and standards are public, explicit and understood. Failure to articulate requirements makes conformity impossible. It is therefore necessary to implement a range of strategies which make quality intrinsic to every operation.

1. Quality policy

This is driven by the school's mission; it is a declaration of hope, aspiration and ambition and it spells out what quality means. The components of a quality policy might include:

- a definition of quality for the school;
- the systems to be applied;
- customer orientation;
- respect for the individual;
- the significance of training and development;
- management commitment;
- responsibility for quality.

2. Operating procedures

Many of the problems that occur in schools are due to a breakdown in working procedures. This is the fault of managers whose responsibility it is to ensure that operating procedures are clear, understood and capable of implementation. The failure of a process says more about the system and its designer than the people who operated it. Schools often have published procedures for basic processes, e.g. marking registers – however, if a process is significant (and if it is not, why continue it?) then it requires an operating procedure. The best examples of operating procedures in schools are syllabuses and schemes of work.

Operating procedures are appropriate for:

- marking, recording and assessment;
- managing pastoral care issues;
- relationships with external bodies – police, social services etc;
- health and safety issues;
- record keeping;
- consultative procedures;
- homework;
- stock control;
- applying for courses;
- disciplinary matters;
- parents' evenings;
- option arrangements;
- handling finance;
- planning trips;
- transfer to secondary school, post-compulsory education.

There is obviously a danger that itemising procedures in detail could become a bureaucratic nightmare and if such documents are just issued then they will probably be ignored. However, if the development of these procedures is managed as a quality process in itself then they are likely to pervade all aspects of school life. In order to achieve this, procedures need to be developed and improved by the teams that will implement them and they must be written in response to customer requirements. In some instances there will be legal obligations on teachers but in many cases writing the procedures will be a first step towards customer satisfaction. Producing the procedures is a classic example of delegation and trust in action and those who write them will need training.

Once produced the procedures should be an essential component of working life, constantly referred to, used in meetings and as a standard reference point. This means that they should be well produced, meeting teachers' and non-teachers' needs in terms of language, design and organisation. They might well take the form of a handbook which includes the mission statement, quality policy and job descriptions of *all* those employed in the school.

The handbook will thus become an essential component of induction, appraisal and development and will provide support for teachers, managers and governors in a wide range of personnel procedures.

3. Quality criteria

These may well form part of operating procedures; they are necessary to identify exactly the standard of work required – in essence procedures will identify who? what? and when? and the quality criteria will indicate how?. For example the National Curriculum will specify the content, sequencing and level of a topic, a school's quality criteria will identify the resources to be used, the strategies to be employed, the subject and methods of assessment. The concern here is with consistency of practice and ensuring that every process is delivered to the optimum quality.

One of the most important applications of quality criteria is in the appraisal and staff development policy of a school. Criteria are essential components of the self-review, classroom and task observation and target setting processes. There are two central issues here: firstly the appraisal and development process is designed to recognise and reinforce the successes of the teacher and identify development needs. Those needs must be met in accordance with the mission and development plan of the school which are expressed in the quality criteria. Secondly the management of the appraisal and professional development processes must, of themselves, be quality processes, i.e. quality can only be achieved by delivering quality. The medium is the message.

The implementation of the School Teacher Appraisal Regulations will necessitate the development of criteria for appraisal; it is suggested that the following areas need to be covered:

- relationships with children;
- lesson planning and preparation;
- organisation of the classroom and resources;
- classroom management;
- assessment and monitoring of pupils' progress;
- subject knowledge;
- pastoral care;
- departmental management;
- .leadership.

The detailed components of each of these areas need to take into account DES, LEA and diocesan requirements, the provisions of the Education Acts and the community in which the school works.

4. Monitoring and review

It is important to distinguish between monitoring and inspection in the context of TQM and inspection in the LEA/school context. A TQM organisation strives to eliminate inspection as manifested in quality control (see Chapter 2). HMI and LEAs have a statutory responsibility to inspect schools. In some senses the notion of external inspection is alien to a quality management approach unless advisers and HMI are seen as clients/customers who have rights and duties which the school has to meet.

Therefore it is not inspection in the sense of *post-facto* fault finding but rather a process of obtaining feedback and advice from two major customers (DES and LEA) on the extent to which requirements are being met.

Within the school, monitoring and review are implicit to every school process, e.g. appraisal team meetings, budget planning, school development plans etc. The important thing is that the process of monitoring and review should be carried out by those actually responsible for the process and that it should become implicit to the way of working. A number of review techniques are outlined in section 3 of this chapter. As far as possible the review process should be specific and focus on the question, 'To what extent have customer requirements been met?' Monitoring should be a regular component of all processes which in time can contribute to a review, i.e. an overview of how they are contributing to the achievement of the school's mission statement.

The cost of quality

One of the great myths surrounding traditional views of quality is
that it costs more. This is understandable if quality is viewed as
'goodness' – as an intangible which has to be struggled for. If
goodness is the top of the mountain then it is obvious that the greater
the energy expended the better the chance of getting to the top.
However, an analysis of the map might reveal a better route,
planning and preparation will maximise the distance covered –
appropriate equipment will ease the journey – a greater distance can
be covered with less output of energy. Even with the right
equipment a wrong turning means wasted effort, having to retrace
the journey and start again. Getting it right first time means the
objective is achieved at minimum cost.

It takes time, money, effort, skill and knowledge to produce
defective services. No manager or teacher in a school will deliberately waste resources, yet a great deal of time will be spent
'reworking', checking and inspecting, all of which are symptomatic
of waste. No amount of additional expenditure will improve a faulty
system or process, the process itself has to be modified in response to
client needs. Figure 4.3 provides a basis for analysing the extent to
which non-conformance to customer specifications is responsible for
wasted resources of time, skills etc. Every positive response indicates
waste. The greater the total the higher the waste and the lower the
level of customer satisfaction.

It is not appropriate to blame the person involved, the chances
are that they did not conform to requirements because the process
was not understood, was inappropriate or badly designed in the first
place. The best way to overcome this problem is to redesign the
process to ensure that it is driven by customer requirements. This
will in turn ensure a higher probability of conformity and thus the
delivery of quality.

The traditional approach is demonstrated in Figure 4.4 (A);
quality is perceived as costing more in proportion to the reducing
number of defects. There is therefore an optimum point after which
improving quality means increased costs to customers and thus
reduced demand. This approach is symptomatic of many western
companies and explains their decline relative to their Japanese
competitors. It might also help to indicate why two schools with the
same budget, serving similar communities achieve remarkably
different outcomes. In essence it is delivering more for the same
input.

Select a short time-span, a week or a fortnight and identify the number of times you have had to do each activity.

Activity	
Doing the same job twice	
Having work retyped	
Postpone a meeting	
Ask for clarification of a document	
Reset deadlines	
Provide 'on the spot' training	
Seek more information	
Modify printed material	
Ask for an agenda	
Clarify the purpose of a task	
Ask for work to be repeated	
Seek confirmation of a verbal agreement	
Explain documentation	
Ask for more time	
Find spare accommodation	
Confirm an order	
Change a timetable	
Duplicate information	
Get equipment repaired	
Leave a job half-finished	
Take over a delegated task	
Redefine specifications	
Return wrongly ordered goods	
'Cut corners'	
Abandon agreed procedures.	

Figure 4.3 Understanding the cost of non-conformance

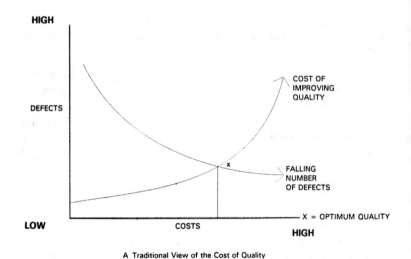

A Traditional View of the Cost of Quality

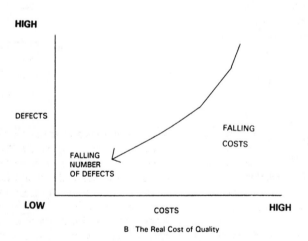

B   The Real Cost of Quality

Figure 4.4   Views of the cost of quality (MacDonald and Piggott, 1990)

The actual cost of quality is shown in Figure 4.4 (B); reducing errors, and thereby waste, cuts costs. The formula is very simple, reduced errors equal increased customer satisfaction equal improved quality. Crosby (1979) makes this point most forcibly in his book *Quality is Free*. Investment is not necessary to improve quality, managing processes are, and that involves doing the right things, i.e. ensuring conformance.

There is very little empirical research on waste in schools. The figure that is often quoted for manufacturing industry in the west is 25 per cent of sales revenue. In service industries the figure may be 30 to 40 per cent of operating costs. It is difficult to speculate what such a figure might be in schools but if it is only 10 per cent of non-staffing costs then it represents a highly significant amount of money. If the principle is extended to staffing costs then the implications are alarming. The following are possible areas for investigating waste:

- all meetings;
- INSET days, short and award bearing courses;
- inappropriate textbooks;
- underutilised equipment;
- the stationery store;
- parents' evenings;
- photocopying;
- appointment procedures;
- the allocation of promoted posts;
- use of information technology;
- distribution of capitation;
- timetabling;
- layout of the school.

Readers will be able to add their own categories and then reflect on the potential for waste. For example: an INSET day is a waste unless it leads to change, the stationery store may be full of stock that will not be used for six months – that is a waste of the potential of that money. Photocopying is necessary but teacher time spent copying is wasted. Is capitation allocated on the basis of the School Development Plan and the attainment of learning objectives or on a spurious notion of fairness? Do teachers spend hours writing out lesson notes in longhand and then have them word processed doubling the time needed to produce them?

These examples will doubtless be recognised by many and dismissed as 'that's the way schools are'. However, confirmation is not vindication. The cost of teacher time spent photocopying would probably amount to far more than the cost of employing a copier operator, thus releasing professional 'quality' time.

It may take many years to see the results of working to eliminate waste especially in the intangibles of the education process. However, there are many areas where direct benefits will be almost immediate, not least in enhanced customer satisfaction and increased commitment from those involved in the process. The next section in this chapter describes techniques for measuring and improving work processes.

Techniques for improving work processes

In this section a variety of techniques are described which are designed to help measure and structure techniques to improve work processes. Some are quantitative, others are structured in such a way as to facilitate analysis of complex situations. None of these techniques are new to schools, all have been used, if not always in the manner described. In the context of quality management they are not so much techniques to be employed as ways of working. It is important to place them in the context of effective team functioning, to see them as skills and tools which facilitate a team approach. All of these approaches require practice and review in order to work effectively.

The techniques described are:

1. Benchmarking.
2. Brainstorming.
3. Cause and effect diagram.
4. Five 'hows', five 'whys'.
5. Force field analysis.
6. Measurement charts.
7. Pareto analysis.
8. Problem solving techniques.
9. Readiness and capability.

1. Benchmarking

This is one of the most widely used techniques in TQM organisations and is essentially an exercise in comparative analysis. In the commercial sector it is examining a competitor's product to establish in what ways they are better, or worse, test the quality and examine customer satisfaction.

Benchmarking already takes place in education – it is one of the principal reasons for attending courses and conferences and reading the educational press. In essence it is about finding good ideas and ways to improve existing practice. However, it may be more appropriate to adapt a more systematic and detailed approach. This process works best with a specialist team although it may well draw on the experience and expertise of a range of teams.

Aim: To improve on best practice.

Step 1   Review

- Identify the process or product to be improved.
- Identify those who 'do it better'.
- Gather hard data to inform analysis.

Step 2   Analysis

- What factors contribute to their success?
- Is their product/approach right for us?
- What are the implications of adopting their approach?

Step 3   Planning

- What can we achieve?
- How are we going to achieve these outcomes?

Step 4   Action

- Implement specific actions.
- Monitor progress against norms.
- Go back to the original and review.
- Consider ways of extending improvement.

This process can be carried out on the basis of good practice in different schools. However, it is likely to be more effective within a school. What happens in other teams, departments and classrooms is lkely to be a powerful source of improvement. Internal benchmarking has the additional advantage of helping and supporting review and development processes.

2.   Brainstorming

This is a technique used to generate the maximum number of insights and involve all members of the work team on equal terms. It is particularly powerful in generating solutions to apparently intractable problems and in situations where creativity is at a premium. Brainstorming optimises the range of possible solutions and produces lists of ideas that can be evaluated, prioritised and rank ordered. The technique can be used several times in succession, e.g. (1) problem identification, (2) solution generation, (3) implementation strategy.

Brainstorming works best in groups of 5–10. The process should be managed by a facilitator (not necessarily the team leader) and each session should last from 10–20 minutes.

Step 1

- The problem or issue being reviewed is written on a flip chart or black board.
- Each member of the team suggests ideas which are written up without alteration or comment.
- The facilitator encourages each member of the team to contribute as many ideas as possible.
- The following 'rules' are applied at this stage:

  1. No criticisms or judgements.
  2. No evaluation.
  3. No discussion.
  4. No problem solving.
  5. Anything goes! All ideas are valid.
  6. Everybody is asked for one more idea.

Step 2

The facilitator takes each suggestion in turn and checks with all members of the team to ensure understanding and accuracy of recording.

Step 3

The ideas generated are reviewed for duplication, trivia, the impracticable and inappropriate. Team consensus is needed before any factor is abandoned.

The ideas that are left are now subject to evaluation by applying criteria to them. Criteria might include cost (e.g. a specified limit), staff availability, training required, feasibility, consistency with agreed strategies. Again the team's view on the 'best fit' should prevail.

Step 4

The outcomes that meet all the criteria are potential solutions which may be self-selecting or require further discussion in order to produce a rank-order.

3. Cause and effect diagram

This technique is also known as fishboning or an Ishikawa diagram after the Japanese management writer who developed it (see Figure 4.5). It is one of the most widely used techniques in quality circles and one of the most powerful diagnostic and team development activities. In some respects it resembles brainstorming but is more structured and focused.

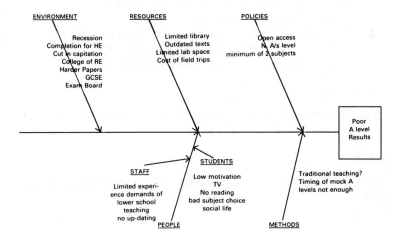

Figure 4.5 Cause and effect diagram

The process can be used to identify the causes of a problem by structuring and displaying them in relation to each other; analysing a process by reviewing factors which may be problematic. The systematic application of a cause and effect diagram can:

- identify *all* the causes of a problem;
- distinguish causes from symptoms;

- analyse the relative significance of related causes;
- provide data for use with other techniques.

The cause and effect approach works best with an established work team led by a facilitator. A maximum of one hour should be spent on the process.

Step 1

Display the diagram (Figure 4.5) on a flip chart, OHP transparency or black/white board. State the problem briefly at the 'head' of the fish. Decide what the characteristics of the 'ribs' should be. It may be helpful to select the most relevant from the list below:

- methods, procedures and stages in the process;
- materials, resources used directly or indirectly;
- people, skills and knowledge;
- measurement, the availability of appropriate data;
- environment, factors influencing the process;
- policies, the principles informing the process.

Step 2

Using brainstorming techniques generate the causes of the problem placing each on the appropriate rib.

Step 3

The facilitator checks understanding with each member of the group.

Step 4

The diagram is analysed for duplication, ambiguities and inappropriate categorisation. Corrections are made.

Step 5

Team members are asked to identify those factors which they perceived to be least significant. Depending on the total number generated 2, 3, 4 or 5 low priorities might be asked for. Those that receive the most 'votes' are deleted.

Step 6

Team members are asked to select the most significant factors (number to be determined by the total available) and to prioritise them. 'Votes' are again collected and the outcome recorded on the diagram.

The process has thus identified possible causes, categorised them, reviewed their relative significance and produced a prioritised list of causes.

Note, For some issues, and for large groups, the diagram can be physically constricting. In this case Step 1 could take the following form:

Members of the group are asked to note down their contributions and the facilitator then goes round the group recording each contribution on flip chart paper and numbering it. The process is continued until all contributions have been recorded. The sheets of paper are displayed and Steps 3-6 above are used in the same way.

This approach can also be used to generate and prioritise solutions to a problem, i.e. it is a more sophisticated form of brainstorming. The topic is the problem to be solved and the team are asked to generate possible solutions which are in turn prioritised and reviewed.

This approach is a version of nominal group technique.

4. Five 'hows', five 'Whys'

These are the same techniques with a different focus. In both cases the idea is to explore a problem or solution until it is expressed in the simplest, most basic terms. In essence a team, with facilitator, examines 'how?' or 'why?' and each proposal is then subjected to further questioning until the root cause is felt to have been reached.

This technique can be exasperating and needs skilled facilitating but it is a powerful tool to overcome superficial responses.

Example

We need to extend the working life of textbooks.

How?
By encouraging children to take better care of them.

How?
By making them personally responsible for them.

How?
By introducing a better monitoring scheme.

How?

By designating someone as being responsible.

How?

By HOD reviewing job descriptions and negotiating the new responsibility.

   Each stage of the process can generate a number of alternatives, each is followed through to the point where an individual accepts responsibility to act to produce a specific outcome within a specified time scale.

5. Force field analysis

Force field analysis helps a team to understand the context in which it is operating and to target those factors which are working in its favour and those which are opposing change. FFA is derived from the premise that any change is subject to *driving forces* which will move it forward and *restraining forces* which will hinder. The technique can be used to analyse the existing situation, identify and build on strengths, identify and minimise restraints. FFA often centres around perceptions and feelings. However, as these are often the most important factors influencing behaviour in organisations they should be given high significance.

Step 1

The facilitator agrees with the group the topic to be analysed – this might be generated by brainstorming or the cause and effect process.

Step 2

Each member of the team is asked to work individually using the FFA sheet (Figure 4.6).

Step 3

The facilitator manages the process of identifying, agreeing, prioritising and recording the team's perceptions. Several drafts of the team diagram may be necessary. Perceptions of the relative strength and significance of each topic can be indicated by the relative size of arrows, placed on the continuum or listed according to priority.

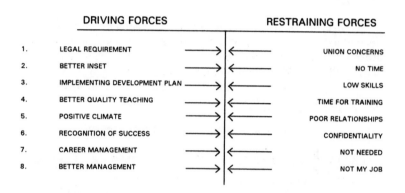

IMPLEMENTING TEACHER APPRAISAL

	DRIVING FORCES			RESTRAINING FORCES
1.	LEGAL REQUIREMENT	⟶	⟵	UNION CONCERNS
2.	BETTER INSET	⟶	⟵	NO TIME
3.	IMPLEMENTING DEVELOPMENT PLAN	⟶	⟵	LOW SKILLS
4.	BETTER QUALITY TEACHING	⟶	⟵	TIME FOR TRAINING
5.	POSITIVE CLIMATE	⟶	⟵	POOR RELATIONSHIPS
6.	RECOGNITION OF SUCCESS	⟶	⟵	CONFIDENTIALITY
7.	CAREER MANAGEMENT	⟶	⟵	NOT NEEDED
8.	BETTER MANAGEMENT	⟶	⟵	NOT MY JOB

Figure 4.6 Force field analysis

Step 4

The team agrees on the driving forces to be reinforced and the restraining forces to be overcome. The two elements can often be correlated and a readiness and capability chart (see below) used to target specific actions.

6. Measurement charts

This is a method of giving graphic representation to trends to facilitate analysis, identify nonconformance, create common understanding and measure change over time. This process can be used for a variety of purposes and helps to maximise the possibility of objective analysis. The process should not be seen as an attempt to quantify for its own sake but rather to help the process of measurement.

The first step is to identify an individual to be responsible for managing the process. According to the process to be measured, the criteria to be applied, the unit of measurement and the timescale to be used should all be agreed. In many school processes attaching numerical values may be problematic but in fact teachers are expert at translating children's work into grades and there is considerable experience in the evaluation of INSET courses!

Example

It has been decided to review senior management team meetings over a half-term period. The key components of a succesful meeting are agreed and each team member completes the review sheet (kept simple) at the end of each meeting. The scores are aggregated and recorded and the reasons used as the basis for review, analysis and implementation of changes.

Senior management team meeting – review

Please rate each category below for this meeting. 1 = poor, unsatisfactory; 10 = excellent.

1.	Agenda received in advance	1 2 3 4 5 6 7 8 9 10
2.	Meeting kept to time	1 2 3 4 5 6 7 8 9 10
3.	Documentation/data available	1 2 3 4 5 6 7 8 9 10
4.	Decisions taken	1 2 3 4 5 6 7 8 9 10
5.	Actions agreed	1 2 3 4 5 6 7 8 9 10
6.	Full participation	1 2 3 4 5 6 7 8 9 10
7.	Appropriate leadership	1 2 3 4 5 6 7 8 9 10
8.	Planning and review sessions	1 2 3 4 5 6 7 8 9 10

A crucial decision is to establish a goal-line – a standard which is regarded as the optimum to be achieved. For some processes this may be arbitrary but experience will identify proper levels.

The measurement chart for the team meeting could appear as in Figure 4.7. The chart displays relative satisfaction and provides a focus for analysis. Individual scores may be displayed as a means of generating discussion and involving all team members in the analysis of the factors leading to dissatisfaction.

This technique has the advantage of being simple and im-mediate, the discussion generated is more significant than the statistical validity of the method.

7. *Pareto analysis*

This technique helps to establish the vital elements of a problem

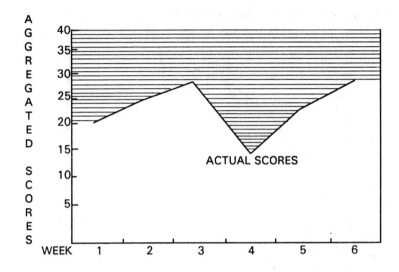

The disparity between the actual score and the possible score is the cost of non-conformance. The objective to reduce that cost.

Figure 4.7 Measurement chart SMT meetings

from the relatively trivial. The approach is derived from the work of the Italian economist Pareto who put forward the '80/20' hypothesis, i.e. 80 per cent of the problems are caused by 20 per cent of the process. Pareto analysis is a means of identifying the *real* cause of the problem so that it can be addressed directly.

Step 1

Identify the problems to be compared by brainstorming or cause and effect analysis. Identify an appropriate unit of measurement and specify a time period for getting data.

Step 2

Gather results and display them using a histogram. Re-order the histogram so that it displays declining frequency from left to right.

Step 3

Label the right-hand vertical axis to show the cumulative percentage of the total distribution as in Figure 4.8.

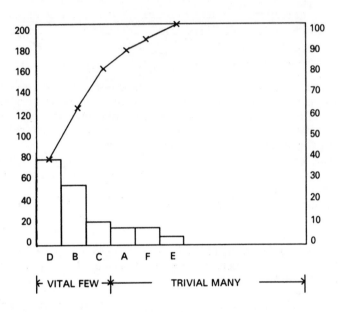

REPORTED PROBLEMS

A   -   Corrections/spelling mistakes
B   -   Not completed on time
C   -   Incomplete comments
D   -   No envelopes
E   -   Inappropriate comments
F   -   Shortage of forms.

Pareto analysis of the factors resulting in reports being sent out late.

Figure 4.8   Pareto analysis

In the example shown in Figure 4.8 two factors account for two thirds of the late reports. It is therefore possible to identify appropriate remedial activity which is specifically targeted. It also becomes possible to analyse the extent to which the problem has been overcome on future occasions. Although the result might be guessed intuitively the Pareto analysis ensures that the response meets the real need and provides evidence to ensure that future monitoring is effective. It also allows for a further stage of analysis to examine the factors causing the 'vital few' problems.

8. Problem solving techniques

A rational, methodical approach to problem solving increases the probability that the problem will be solved with the most appropriate solution. A diagnostic approach is more likely to result in high quality outcomes. It is important to see problem solving as a skill to be developed rather than depend on intuition.

The intuitive response starts from the recognition of the problem, tries to identify causes and then proposes solutions. The outcomes of this approach will include:

- solving the symptoms but not the problem;
- solving the problem but at high cost;
- solving the problem but creating others;
- not solving the problem or the symptoms but learning to live with both.

In a quality environment none of these outcomes is acceptable. The real problem must be solved (thereby removing the symptoms); the solution must not increase costs and must be capable of full implementation.

The components of a rational approach to problem solving are shown in Figure 4.9.

- Identification: This stage involves identifying the actual problem to be solved, i.e. not the symptoms but the core cause. In order to do this it is necessary to specify as many different aspects and components as possible. Techniques such as brainstorming, Pareto analysis, 'five whys' and cause and effect are appropriate at this stage.
  Once the problem has been identified it needs to be 'unpacked', i.e. to be further defined by distinguishing cause and effect; Pareto analysis and 'five whys' are appropriate here.
- Diagnosis: Having identified the actual problem to be solved then systematic analysis of the causes is possible. Brainstorming and cause and effect analysis are appropriate. Once hypotheses have been developed they can be tested using

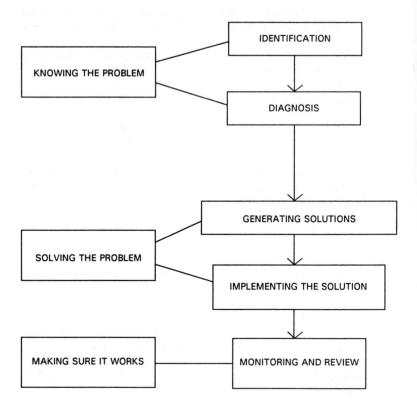

Figure 4.9 The rational approach to problem solving

    measurement charts, Pareto analysis or active experiment-
ation depending on the nature of the issue. At this stage it
should be possible to identify the root cause.
- Generating solutions: The first stage here is to generate as
    many solutions as possible – brainstorming is obviously a
    powerful technique in this context or nominal group tech-
    niques could be used, the 'five hows' may well be most
    appropriate. Once the options have been identified then it is
    appropriate to employ team based consensus decision making
    techniques.

- Implementation: Once the optimum solution has been identified then it is vital to move to implementation. Force field analysis and readiness and capability are appropriate prerequisites to action. The actual solution should be expressed in terms similar to those concerned with delegation and effective teams – most importantly setting targets specific to named individuals in a clear time scale with appropriate resources and authority.
- Monitoring and review: Monitoring is necessary to ensure that the chosen solution is actually working. Immediate feedback will be obtained by using the same techniques that originally defined the problem. More specifically measurement charts can be employed to allow comparative data to be generated, interviewing those involved can also provide instant feedback. Longer term review is required for two reasons; firstly to ensure that the solution is institutionalised, i.e. it becomes part of the way of working. Secondly it is important to review the problem solving process itself to ensure that it was cost effective and enhanced team skills.

9. Readiness and capability

The purpose of this activity is to analyse and increase understanding of the individuals involved in a process in terms of their:

- readiness, i.e. their motivation, capability commitment and willingness to be involved;
- capability, i.e. their knowledge, skills, influence and potential positive or negative power.

This is an individual activity but can usually be carried out by a small team.

The individuals likely to be significant in a particular process are identified and their readiness and capability are then plotted (see Figure 4.10). On the basis of an individual's location on the grid it is possible to identify a range of strategies.

On the basis of the analysis shown in Figure 4.10 AW is clearly a significant person and should be fully involved from the outset. Those with high readiness and low capability clearly need support, development and training. Those with low readiness and high capability need to be involved and motivated to ensure that they do not become negative forces. The potential weakness of this approach (high subjectivity) can be overcome by sharing perceptions, e.g. by each member of the team completing the grid in respect of the other

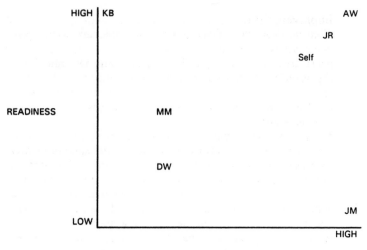

Readiness and Capability chart for introducing a new approach
to science teaching.
(initials refer to teachers involved)

Figure 4.10   Readiness and capability

members and pooling and sharing perceptions. This will often
facilitate openness about attitudes and can be a powerful team
development activity.

Summary

- Managing quality is about measurement.
- All work is a process.
- Managing processes is about adding value.
- School processes can be measured.
- Prevention is better than inspection.
- Prevention is achieved through operating procedures.
- Improving quality means reducing costs.
- Quality is free.
- Techniques for improving processes are readily available.

Action

- Start calculating the cost of non-conformance.
- Analyse work processes in school and identify ways of

improving them.
- Identify examples of waste, calculate the cost and improve the process.
- Start using the techniques for improving work processes.
- Analyse your behaviour in terms of:

  - the clarity of the specifications you give;
  - the amount of 'hassle' in your life;
  - the amount of time spent reworking;
  - the amount of time spent dealing with problems, complaints and grievances.

5 Mission and planning

Virtually all schools will have published a set of aims – a set of statements about the values and principles which are the basis of the school's working life. The aims will probably be published in the 'Handbook for Staff' (if there is one) and the 'School Prospectus'. Some schools may also publish an accompanying list of objectives, but these are often indistinguishable from the aims.

Analysis of a school's aims will usually reveal entirely proper, appropriate and valid sentiments. However, in the context of quality management a number of questions have to be asked about the traditional approach to aims and their relationship to planning:

Who wrote the aims?
When were they written?
When were they last revised?
Do all those that they affect know and accept them?
Are they used as criteria for evaluation?
Do they inform all management processes?
Are they written in meaningful language?
Is any attempt made to measure the extent to which they are achieved?

Mission

Successful schools have explicit values which are shared by all members of the school community, explained to all those who come into contact with the school and used as the basis for all aspects of the life of the school. Successful schools know where they are going and how they are going to get there. Values which are implicit are not capable of implementation. There is therefore a need to translate the values which inform the management of a school into a public and shared statement which is a public commitment to the core purpose. Such a statement is usually referred to as the mission.

The mission statement serves a number of practical purposes:

- It characterises the school to its community.
- It provides a sense of direction and purpose.
- It serves as a criterion for policy making.
- It sets the school culture.
- It generates consistency of action.
- It identifies clients.
- It serves to motivate and challenge.

Above all the mission statement creates a sense of uniqueness and identity which also serves as a platform for action. A mission statement has the same function as a motto or badge – it is a label which is instantly recognisable and sends an unequivocal statement about values and purpose. The mission statement equally indicates what the school wants to succeed in; what it does and does not do and, crucially, how it seeks to do it. It then becomes possible to apply an instant test of validity and relevance to any proposed change – to what extent is this proposal change consistent with our core purpose? A mission statement makes explicit the values of a school and therefore does much to indicate the expectations as to what the culture of the school should be. This in turn facilitates the development of operating procedures which translate principle into practice. Mission statements inform the writing of objectives which will inform budgetary planning, staff development and curriculum planning. Equally they set the context for the writing of management procedures, job descriptions, schemes of work etc. By relating these means of implementation back to the mission statement, consistency is possible. The statement also needs to specify clients so that the responsibility to provide a quality service is a permanent feature of activity in the school.

Finally, mission statements are about challenge, excitement and giving meaning to work. They help to set the routine, the mundane and the ordinary in the context of the broader purpose and the drive for continuous improvement.

The well written mission statement thus acts as a bridge between the values, vision and moral purpose of a school on the one hand and practical activity and implementation on the other.

In order to fulfil the functions identified above, mission statements need to have the following components:

statements need to have the following components:

- an indication of the core purpose;
- a clear statement of relationships with clients;
- specification of the services to be provided;
- explicit reference to values;
- a commitment to quality;
- a concern for employees.

There is no rubric as to the most appropriate length of a mission statement, it may be no more than 25–30 words, it may be significantly longer. The crucial thing is that it is understandable to those who have to implement it and that it is capable of implementation. Above all the mission statement should display fitness for purpose, i.e. it should meet the practical needs of school managers. The statement should therefore link a range of factors to inform and influence management activity. Figure 5.1 suggests the context of a mission statement.

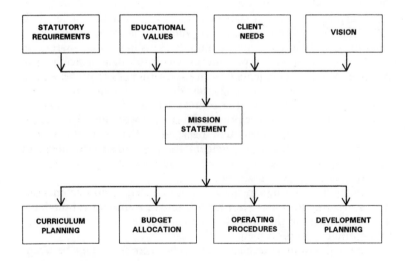

Figure 5.1   The context of the mission statement

The process of producing a mission statement is as significant as the statement itself. The level of involvement, consultation and shared decision making will do much to make the statement operative. It is equally important that the process should reflect the principles outlined in the statement. In essence, the greater the involvement the higher the quality of the statement and the greater the potential commitment. *Ex cathedra* statements which are handed down are unlikely to function as the source of vision and motivation.

However, vision by committee seems unlikely to work, so considerable care has to be exercised in managing the process of developing a mission statement. There are three main stages to producing a mission statement: planning, writing and reviewing. Each stage is time consuming, intellectually demanding and requires significant skills of team work, collaborative decision making and problem solving. Writing a mission statement is thus both an essential prerequisite to implementing a quality management policy and an example of such a process. The natural focus for initiating and sustaining the process is the senior management team. However the impact of a mission statement is directly related to the involvement of those it will affect and those who will have to implement it. The use of a project team approach may well be the most appropriate.

Planning the statement

Preparation for the production of a mission statement is essential as failure may be more counter-productive than never starting. The issues to be considered by senior managers can be best expressed in a series of questions:

1. Does the current situation demand a fundamental re-appraisal of the school's management values?
2. Do the benefits of a mission statement justify the time and energy required?
3. Will what we do make a real difference?
4. Is there something important to be said about our management values and practices that will influence the future of the school?
5. Can we afford to invest the time?
6. Can we afford not to invest the time?
7. How objective and honest can we be about our management practices and relationships?
8. Are we prepared to seek and accept feedback from all our clients?

9. Do we have the skills necessary to initiate and sustain the process?
10. Are we prepared to implement, work by and be judged by the statement we produce?

Unless the answer to these questions is unequivocal, then it may well be that there are other issues to be considered first. In the case of a senior management team it may well be that a process of systematic team building is necessary (see Chapter 8). Equally significant is the perception of the headteacher. Unless she or he has formulated a clear view of her/his personal expectations and values and is able and willing to communicate them to maximum effect then the process of developing a mission statement will not work.

The second stage of the planning process is to establish the context that will inform the implementation of the mission statement. This is a complex process of identification, clarification and prioritisation which may well require use of the techniques outlined in Chapter 3. The variables to be considered will change from school to school but may include:

-   Statutory requirements – notably the demands of the Education Reform Act 1988 and associated legislation.
-   LEA policies and procedures.
-   The views of children, parents and employers.
-   The views of the governing body.
-   The perspectives of teaching and non-teaching staff.
-   The views of LEA advisers, officers and others with whom the school has regular dealings.
-   Documentary evidence:

    -   HMI and LEA inspection reports;
    -   whole school review (e.g. GRIDS and DION);
    -   evaluation and monitoring reports;
    -   reports to the governing body;
    -   statistical data.

This data will do much to identify current views and attitudes, needs and expectations. However, a mission statement should not be simply descriptive but should also be concerned with the future, with aspirations and building on success. This requires articulating the vision. This can be done in a number of ways.

1. Celebrating strengths
    Each person involved is asked to identify the strengths of the

school, the aspects of its work and life that are most worthy of recognition and celebration and then to specify the factors which contribute to the success.

2. Envisioning
   Individuals are asked to envision the ideal state for the school in five or ten years' time – what sort of place should the school be? How should it feel?

3. Client orientation
   Members of the project team complete the phrases:
   'If I were a parent considering sending my child to this school I would want....'
   'If I were a child at this school I would want....'

4. Clarifying values
   'In this school we really care about....'

Each of these exercises generates a range of values and principles that are essentially personal. However this reflects the reality of any organisation – it is the sum of individual perceptions. The important thing is to aggregate these individual perceptions so that they are shared and refined into a collective view, the highest common factor. Significant and fundamental as these views and values are, they need to be set in the context of anticipated and known changes which will influence the school; what might be termed the 'hard' data, e.g.:

- What are the demographic trends influencing the school's recruitment?
- What impact will the implementation of the National Curriculum have?
- How will the continuing implementation of LMS influence the school's resource base?
- What are the likely changing needs of other schools, higher and further education and employers?
- What is the age and qualifications profile of the staff of the school? How will this affect curriculum provision?
- Do we have any identifiable weaknesses to redress?
- How appropriate are training and development strategies for staff?
- Are management structures and procedures appropriate?

The clarification of values and expectations coupled with an analysis of the context in which the school will be operating provide the raw data for the production of the mission statement. The statement is then a valid basis for the writing of a development plan. The relationship may be illustrated as shown in Figure 5.2.

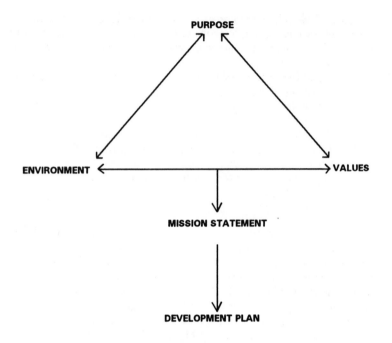

Figure 5.2   Mission and strategy

Writing the statement

Once all values and expectations have been expressed and collected, and as much data has been collected as is reasonably available, then it is possible to write the mission statement. There are two issues to be considered in the writing process; firstly it is a complex process involving significant skills in synthesising complex issues and adopting appropriate language. The quality of 'conformity to requirements' is particularly apposite here – who is going to use the document and for what purposes should determine its language and layout. It should not be seen as an opportunity for intellectual 'one-upmanship' but rather a real, relevant and usable document. Secondly the actual writing process needs to be carefully managed so as to ensure commitment and enhance relationships.

There is a tension between the practical demands of producing the statement and ensuring maximum involvement and creativity. No committee has yet written a sonnet. The writing process is probably best handled by the project team with a consultant/

facilitator. The role of the consultant is to help achieve a product in a reasonable timescale whilst constantly questioning, checking and reminding the team of its task and the context in which it is operating.

Once a first draft is produced it can be tested by the team by using the following check-lists:

Process:

1. Were you able to make a full contribution?
2. Were you listened to?
3. Did anyone in the team block your ideas?
4. Was the team creative?
5. Was the team realistic?
6. Did the team hold on to the fundamental purpose of the school?
7. Has the team resolved ambiguities and uncertainties?
8. Are you personally fully committed to the mission statement?

Outcome:

Your mission statement will not work if it is:

- written in an alien language;
- a series of pious aspirations;
- a list of outcomes;
- a series of imperatives to staff;
- insensitive to clients' needs;
- too general;
- too prescriptive;
- reinforcing the *status quo*;
- set in a short time-scale;
- reactive and pragmatic;
- lacking senior management commitment.

Assuming that the statement passes the above 'tests' then it should be shown to a cross-section of those whom it is going to affect. They could be asked to comment on its clarity and realism, its comprehensiveness, its acceptability and applicability. Negative responses indicate more work to be done. Positive responses serve as the basis for publication, dissemination and explanation.

Reviewing

Once the mission statement has been published and is a fundamental component of school planning and decision making, its validity will be frequently tested. The review of the school's mission will therefore be a part of all monitoring, inspection and evaluation procedures. However, changes in the environmental factors operating on the school may also necessitate a review of the continuing validity of the statement. Although the central purpose of the school may be immutable the means by which that purpose is achieved will, of necessity, have to be modified. If a mission statement is found to be seriously deficient, is not being used to inform management activity or is irrelevant to the working life of the school then it is probably not a mission statement but rather the views of a minority which have not been made part of the school culture.

The best test of a mission statement is the extent to which it permeates all aspects of school management, how far it becomes the working language of the school and the quality benchmark for all individuals and teams to review their work.

The example of a possible mission statement shown in Figure 5.3 is not intended to be prescriptive but rather to illustrate how the various components identified above might be expressed. It cannot be stressed too strongly that each mission statement must be unique to its school and that the process of producing the statement is a significant event in the implementation of a total quality approach.

Planning

If the mission statement identifies the destination of a school, then planning is necessary to specify the timetable and stops on the journey. No school will achieve quality management through rhetoric and exhortation; values are only given reality through action, and managing is about action rather than contemplation. A mission statement is therefore only valid when it is part of a planning process which translates aspirations into activity and helps each individual see how her/his actions contribute to the attainment of the school's purposes. Planning therefore has to integrate the mission statement into a process which allows individuals to plan and prioritise their own work so the school needs and individual activity are harmonised.

The key process in Figure 5.4 is vectoring – moving from the general to the specific, the abstract to the concrete the common to the personal. It is only when individuals are able to participate in the setting of specific targets that measurable outcomes will occur. In the

MISSION STATEMENT OF XYZ SCHOOL

1.   Our primary purpose is to enhance children's quality of learning through the effective and efficient delivery of the curriculum.

2.   We believe that our first responsibility is to our clients, to meet their needs and to provide outstanding service.

3.   We will provide a range of educational and social experiences appropriate to the age, ability and needs of our pupils.

4.   We will have consistently high expectations and match these with high quality resources and learning strategies.

5.   We are committed to honesty and responsibility in all relationships, respecting the legitimate rights of individuals and stressing the importance of social awareness and sensitivity.

6.   We will create opportunities for every individual in the school community to develop her or his maximum potential.

7.   We will manage resources to ensure maximum educational benefit.

8.   We will create and sustain a professional learning environment.

9.   We will adopt a philosophy of continuous improvement of every aspect of the school's work and life.

Figure 5.3   A model mission statement

MISSION STATEMENT

OBJECTIVES

TARGETS

Figure 5.4   Mission and planning

hierarchy shown in Figure 5.4 objectives are short term (one or two year) school priorities and targets are personal, short term (six months to one year) outcomes. School objectives are established through the development planning process and targets through the appraisal process. The interconnection of mission statement, development planning and target setting is demonstrated in Figure 5.5.

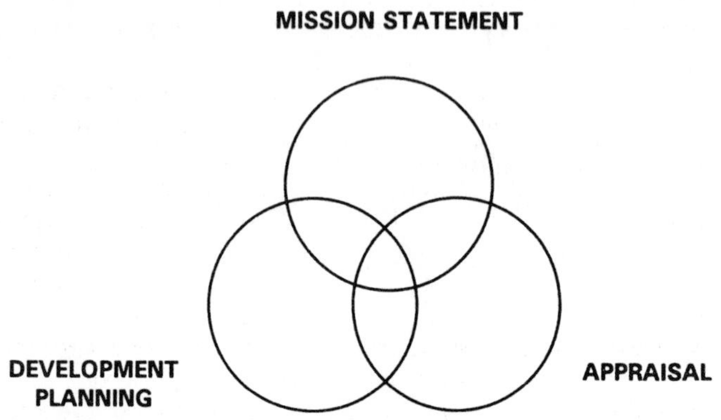

MISSION STATEMENT

DEVELOPMENT   **APPRAISAL**
PLANNING

Figure 5.5   Mission, planning and targets

In this process each component feeds off the other, they are interdependent and inadequacy on the part of one will compromise the other two. At the critical point where the three coincide there is quality in action with values directly influencing behaviour.

Development planning

The planning cycle, in any of its various formulations is now widely known. However, it is important to stress in the context of quality management that the planning process has to be client driven and that the management of the cycle is, in itself, a significant quality issue. This places the mission statement firmly at the outset of the planning process and requires constant reference to it as the criterion for acceptability and prioritisation. Equally significant is the importance of the planning cycle harmonising all components of the management process. Thus the mission statement informs and drives curriculum planning, which in turn informs staff recruitment, deployment and development, which in turn determines the budget. The budgetary process is therefore objective driven rather than being incremental and the quality purpose of the school is the key determinant of decision making.

The principal stages in the planning process may be identified as:

- Setting objectives; translating the broad imperatives of the mission statement into specific outcomes which are attributed to individuals, set within a defined time-scale and with clear performance indicators.
- Allocating resources; ensuring that financial, physical and personal resources are attributed to each objective so as to ensure that it is attainable. There is no merit in setting objectives without allocating the necessary resources. Equally important is deployment of staff with appropriate skills, knowledge and authority.
- Implementation; this requires the translation of the objectives into specific actions by individuals. For this to happen these actions need to be defined in concrete terms with appropriate training and development if necessary. Implementation may be by individuals or through teams.
- Monitoring and evaluation; if objectives have been appropriately written then monitoring is a simple exercise, if performance indicators are written in sufficiently concrete and specific terms then failure or success will be immediately apparent. Evaluation is carried out in the terms of the mission statement, i.e. the extent to which the objectives have enhanced compliance with stated purposes.

Appraisal

Appraisal is a fundamentally significant process in the context of quality management. Appraisal of managers and teachers in schools may be said to have three essential purposes:

1. Recognition and reinforcement of success and consolidation of effective practice.
2. Diagnosis of professional development and training needs.
3. Negotiation of personal targets which identify personal responsibility for the implementation of school objectives.

Appraisal as envisaged by the National Steering Group (1989) and the DES in circular 12/91 (1991) is operated in an hierarchical way. Thus at each stage of the school hierarchy there is a clear responsibility to translate the school's mission and objectives into practical outcomes which lead to change. The way in which this process might operate is illustrated in the following.

Focus from mission statement

We will have consistently high expectations and match these with high quality resources and learning strategies.

School objective 1991/93

To reduce unwarranted absence in year 11 by 50 per cent in the current academic year.

Deputy headteacher's target

To produce a strategy to develop appropriate learning strategies for less able pupils by September 1992 and manage its implementation.

Subject coordinator's target

To review learning resources and teaching strategies and organise the production of appropriate materials for less able students in year 11 and implement changes by January 1993.

Classroom teacher's target

To attend the LEA course on 'History for the less able', present proposals at the following departmental meeting and contribute to the production of flexible learning materials.

At each stage the target becomes more specific and the whole process is underpinned by:

- the allocation of appropriate resources of time, money etc.;
- the provision of appropriate training;
- the existence of clear criteria for acceptable performance.

The aspiration of the mission statement is thus turned into concrete behaviour – the impact of which can be measured and modified if appropriate. By following this process, roles and responsibilities are also clarified and the workload of individuals is managed more effectively. However, this process will only work if the mission statement exists, is written in appropriate terms, has the commitment of all involved and is a living document used at all stages of the management process. Without this integrated approach, aims are likely to remain pious platitudes and planning *ad hoc* and reactive.

Summary

- Quality management requires a mission statement which permeates all aspects of school life.
- The mission statement must be orientated towards the school's clients.
- The mission statement must be understandable, specific and capable of implementation
- The production of a mission statement is the responsibility of senior management.
- The statement must balance vision with realism.
- A mission statement must be written for its audience – not its writers.
- The statement must be constantly communicated.
- *Planning must grow* out of the mission.
- Appraisal is a vehicle for translating principle into practice.

Action

- Review your school aims – do they directly influence your management processes?
- Do your school aims provide a vivid and exciting picture of what your school is all about? If not where does the vision come from?
- Refer to your aims/mission every day. Make them real for all members of the school community.
- Find out if your colleagues' vision is compatible with yours.
- Does your conduct reinforce your school's values?

6 Culture

Culture is one of the least tangible but most significant elements in creating a quality environment. If the culture of a school is not appropriate then the principles outlined in Chapters 2, 3 and 5 will have limited impact and the practical approaches in Chapters 7, 8 and 9 will become superficial rituals. This chapter is therefore a bridge between principles and application. The cultures of schools vary enormously and have a profound and direct impact upon behaviour and performance. The purpose of this chapter is to identify the factors that contribute to a school's culture and the changes that may be necessary to create a 'quality culture'. The following issues are examined:

- defining culture;
- defining a quality culture;
- factors influencing culture.

Defining culture

In simplistic terms an organisation's culture is its personality – the sum of all those elements that add up to make it unique. Culture is the product of the shared values, beliefs, priorities, expectations and norms that serve to inform the way in which an organisation manifests itself to the world. Culture only has meaning when it is given expression, when it is expressed in tangible forms. The critical difference about culture is that it is those abstractions which are *shared*, those which are widely held and dominant. All organisations have multiple sub-sets, localised beliefs which give meaning to particular parts of the whole, however, in the context of quality there needs to be a consistency of purpose, a shared value system which permeates all aspects of organisation and so is manifested in practical terms. There is an obvious tension between the demands of the organisation and the values of the individual. The image of quality management is often a distorted one of oriental uniformity and conformity. The skill in managing cultural change is to generate consensus, to recruit and develop in accordance with the culture and to help those who cannot 'fit' – find an appropriate niche – so that they are fully developed in personal terms.

Describing, defining and illustrating the concept of culture

Charles Handy (1990) has gone further than most to make the issues clear and understandable. Handy has developed the notion of tribes to help define the characteristics that go to make up organisations.

	CLUB	ROLE	TASK	PERSON	CUSTOMER
STRUCTURE	SPIDER'S WEB	PYRAMID	NET	CLUSTER OR CONSTELLATION	CHAIN
FOCUS	THE LEADER	THE STRUCTURE	THE TEAM	THE PERSON	THE CUSTOMER
COMMUNICATION	BASED ON TRUST SHARED UNDERSTANDING	FORMAL BASED ON SYSTEMS AND PROCEDURES	OPEN, RELAXED	PERSONAL	OPEN TWO-WAY
STYLE	PERSONALITY CENTRED HOMOGENEOUS	PREDICTABLE, CERTAIN	CO-OPERATIVE FORWARD LOOKING	TECHNICALLY BASED	OBSESSIVE VALUE DRIVEN, MEASURED
RESPONSIVENESS	RAPID FLEXIBLE	LIMITED, RULE CENTRED	TASK FOCUSED	HIGH	HIGH CONSTANT IMPROVEMENT
EXAMPLES	ARTISTS THEATRE POLITICS	GOVERNMENT DEPARTMENTS	SURGICAL TEAMS, PROJECT GROUPS	DOCTORS, BARRISTERS, ARCHITECTS, UNIVERSITY DEPTS.	ANY TEAM COMPANY OR ORGANISATION

Figure 6.1   Handy's organisational tribes

Figure 6.1 provides a limited summary of Handy's detailed discussion, however, it should be possible to identify schools that conform to each of the tribal definitions. It is possible to caricature schools – the 'club' school with the dominant and all-pervasive headteacher; the 'role' school, the large comprehensive; the 'task' school, often a primary or middle school and the person school, the traditional grammar. In reality of course all schools will contain elements of each tribe. In the secondary school different departments will display different tribal characteristics – the role based science department, the task based English department, the person based art department and the club based PE department.

The issue to be discussed is which of these tribes is appropriate to the quality organisation? The answer is probably not one of them in isolation; all contain elements that are valid, the emphasis on leadership, systems, team work, task focus and high responsiveness all conform to quality criteria. However, this is too random and haphazard so a fifth tribe has been added – with due deference to Professor Handy.

The customer tribe is symbolised by the chain – the tribe only has meaning when it is linked to its suppliers and customers. The focus is totally on the customer – as everyone is a customer. Communication is open and two way and the tribe is motivated by its shared value system. Its responsiveness is total, it only exists to delight its customers. The customer tribe is unusual in that it has invariably evolved from one of the other tribes and traces of early behaviour often emerge. However, the tribe is determined to establish itself in its own right.

Handy also uses the metaphor of classical gods to help analyse the individual's understanding of organisational culture:

- Zeus, works through people by power, operates by strength of personality.
- Apollo, works through harmony and logic, values structure and security.
- Athena, works through excitement, energy problem solving and teams.
- Dionysus, the free spirit, loyal to the craft, intolerant of organisations.

To this distinguished pantheon it is proposed to add Themis. She offered wise counsel to the other gods, she was always helpful and obliging, the goddess of wisdom and justice; she could also vision the future. In these respects she seems ideal as a goddess of quality, especially as she was also revered as a counsellor and a guide for public debate.

Handy's insights provide powerful clues to the components of an organisation's culture. These have been identified in Figure 6.1, i.e. structure, focus, communication, style and responsiveness. Each of these will be significant in its own right; together they will have a profound impact upon the way an organisation actually works as opposed to the intentions or wishes of its leaders and managers. However to understand the practical implications of managing a quality culture it is necessary to translate these conceptual models into the practical aspects of managing in schools. Central to the creation and maintenance of a culture are mission, leadership and teams (dealt with in Chapters 5, 7 and 8 respectively). It is not proposed to repeat the issues identified in these chapters but rather to show how they impact on routine procedures.

Defining a quality culture

If culture is the personality of an organisation then a quality school is restless, constantly questioning, never satisfied, challenging norms and believing that things can always be better. Quality management requires a belief in an infinite capacity for improvement of organisations, processes and people. It is difficult to think of a better environment for such an approach than a school. Schools manage the most complex process of continuous improvement – the growth of children's learning.

Figure 6.1 identified five components of an organisation's culture. The central theme of a quality culture is continuous improvement; the organisation is totally committed to improving all aspects of every activity. There is never a time when there is nothing to be improved, everything is capable of further refinement, further reduction of error and greater customer satisfaction. In terms of the five components this approach has the following manifestations:

Structure

The most powerful image is that of the chain – indeed TQM is often defined as a 'chain of customers'. The image conveys a crucial message of interdependence, the chain being only as strong as the weakest link and only having meaning when the links are firmly interconnected. Quality is integrated into all aspects of the organisation, it permeates every process. Quality management is management, not another activity.

Focus

There is an unequivocal recognition that the organisation exists to serve the customer; it has no other justification. This view is extended to internal and external customers with an emphasis on the external. This means that everyone accepts the responsibility for providing outstanding service – the primary purpose of each job is customer satisfaction. This is managed by constant feedback and measurement.

Communication

Quality organisations give priority to high quality communication, stressing the importance of a constant two way dialogue. Communication is open, frank and purposeful. This is most powerfully demonstrated in the use of autonomous teams which have highly sophisticated internal communication and are able to talk to other teams to direct effect.

Style

The quality organisation is driven by values, not pragmatism or expediency. A long term view is taken with an emphasis on measurement to monitor progress. Crucially everyone in the organisation is obsessed with quality – it permeates language, working procedures and is the criterion used in every activity. High expectations are the norm and are made explicit.

Responsiveness

'The customer is always right' is a cliché but it drives quality organisations: meeting customer needs, as they are expressed is what the organisation exists to do. The emphasis is on prevention not inspection, on delighting the customer by providing superior service and on continuous improvement. A customer complaint triggers action, not resentment or avoidance.

Central to these factors is the behaviour of the leadership of an organisation. For schools to create a quality culture, senior staff must be permanently obsessed with quality. The culture of the school will be a reflection of the head and senior managers and this must be manifested in behaviour, language and imagery. No example of poor quality is ever ignored, all communications refer to quality and all encounters are viewed in terms of their potential to advance quality. However, schools cannot operate by exhortation – the culture of quality needs to permeate all aspects of management processes and practical examples are outlined in the next section.

Factors influencing culture

When anthropologists study a society they derive their conclusions about its culture from observed behaviour. Social behaviour is the means by which culture is most powerfully transmitted (Do as I say or do as I do). Creating a culture appropriate to quality management has to focus on specifics, tangible expression which communicate meaning. In many industrial organisations the first tangible results of a TQM approach have been the abolition of reserved parking spaces, the merging of the executive dining room with the management restaurant and the works canteen and everybody clocking in or nobody clocking in. These are changes that send a direct and uncomplicated message – quality means change in every aspect of working life. More important, the values and mission of the organisation are translated into tangibles which help change understanding and create a new language, new myths and symbols and a view of the reality of the organisation.

Because schools are so diverse and because there can be no stereotype of what makes a 'quality' school the factors influencing quality have to be understood in the specific context of the individual school. The following factors are intended to be generic, but the components of each factor must be identified and determined by the school. Unless they are specific to an individual school, i.e. derived from its mission statement and generated by those working in the school, they are unlikely to be valid or capable of implementation. The issues to be included in such an approach might include:

- Values and mission – the extent to which these are public, shared, understood and acted on.
- Organisational structure – the logic behind the schools hierarchy, the way in which responsibilities are shared, possible duplication of responsibility.
- Communication – the effectiveness of communication within and between work groups and individuals, the quality of information flow.
- Decision making – the amount of real delegation, the quality of decisions, the levels of involvement.
- Working environment – the standards of comfort, cleanliness and suitability for teaching, learning and social interaction.
- Recruitment and selection – the use of appropriate techniques to match people to the culture of the schools and the skills required to do the job.
- Curriculum planning – the timetable, deployment of staff, access to teaching resources.
- Budget and resource management – the extent to which the budget is driven by the curriculum, perceived equity in the allocation of capitation, the availability of resources.
- Pastoral care and discipline – the perceived effectiveness and fairness of pastoral systems.
- Community – the quality of relationships with governors, parents, business, local authorities etc.

An essential precursor to the implementation of a TQM approach is an understanding of the prevailing culture. Attitudinal change will be the foundation of any significant modification of organisational culture, equally the imposition of an 'alien' culture is doomed to failure. A culture 'review' is an essential precursor for two reasons; firstly it provides accurate data for managing the implementation process, secondly it identifies the priorities for action. Figure 6.2 illustrates a school culture review. (It can also inform force field analysis and readiness and capability techniques, see Chapter 4.)

As with all such activities completing the review in isolation may provide insight but is bound to be limited in its potential for action. Aggregating the scores of all interested parties will provide a more powerful basis for analysis, using the review as the basis for team meetings and sharing perceptions which are then translated into actions has the potential to bring about real cultural change. The other chapters of this book all provide insights into the practical aspects of creating a quality culture. Examples are provided below of some of the issues not covered elsewhere.

Organisational structure

Chapter 8 places great emphasis on the team as a crucial component of total quality management. Indeed the team and quality are symbiotic. In planning the implementation of a quality management approach the structure of a school needs to be reviewed in the light of the following questions:

- To what extent does the structure facilitate the functioning of autonomous teams?
- Does the structure reinforce the principles of real and effective delegation?
- How far is the structure a reflection of the school's values and how far an historic, bureaucratic legacy?
- What is the justification for perpetuating an hierarchical structure that diminishes personal responsibility?

One of the most significant features of TQM organisations is the abandonment of formal hierarchies and the reconstitution of the work force in teams. The change from an almost Victorian stratification to teams constituted on the basis of being able to work effectively is one of the most powerful manifestations of cultural change.

As schools become increasingly autonomous in budgeting and staffing terms, so the opportunities are available to move from hierarchies to teams and so give tangible evidence of belief in

Indicate where you perceive your school to be on each continuum:

1.	Values not shared, rarely discussed	1	2	3	4	5 Values real, shared, used
2.	Leaders concerned with procedures	1	2	3	4	5 Leaders involved with people
3.	Complaints a nuisance	1	2	3	4	5 Complaints the basis of growth
4.	Unclear procedures	1	2	3	4	5 Defined Processes
5.	Groups with little sense of purpose	1	2	3	4	5 Self managing teams
6.	Top down communication	1	2	3	4	5 Open, relaxed two way communication
7.	Unilateral decision making	1	2	3	4	5 Collaborative decision making
8.	Parental involvement controlled	1	2	3	4	5 Parents welcomed and integrated
9.	Limited investment in recruiting	1	2	3	4	5 Great care with selection procedures
10.	School environment not cared for	1	2	3	4	5 School environment shows pride and caring
11.	Curriculum planning reactive and pragmatic	1	2	3	4	5 Curriculum planning anticipatory and value driven
12.	Budget planning reactive and incremental	1	2	3	4	5 Budget planning objective driven
13.	Pastoral care marginal and a chore	1	2	3	4	5 Pastoral care implicit to all processes
14.	No monitoring or review	1	2	3	4	5 Constant data collection to improve processes
15.	We get by....	1	2	3	4	5 We are going to be the best school of our type.

Total Score   =

Results :

66 - 75 A total quality school!
56 - 65 The potential for quality
36 - 55 The basis for change is available
 0 - 35 There is a lot to be done

Complete this review with regard to relationships between adults in the school and then with regard to relationships between adults and children.

Figure 6.2   School culture review

democratic processes and equality of opportunity. It has never been easy in schools to demonstrate a precise correlation between pay, status and function.

The implementation of a team approach also provides an opportunity to question the academic/pastoral divide found in many secondary schools. This again raises the issue of the way in which values and mission are put into practice and so create a culture. If the mission of the school is to 'educate the whole child' then it does seem inconsistent to have a structure which compartmentalises that educational process into discreet areas thereby increasing the need for communication, liaison and specialist functions. Many special schools provide a model of an integrated approach to learning and social development.

The demands of the National Curriculum, records of achievement, cross-curricular initiatives and the increasing use of flexible learning all militate against traditional hierarchical compartmentalisation. The organisational practices of small primary schools and special schools may well provide a model: teachers having clearly designated responsibilities for functions over and above their classroom teaching and *leading* the rest of the staff, working as a team, when appropriate. It is becoming increasingly obvious in secondary schools that teachers may be involved in teaching two or even three subjects. As this trend grows the traditional structure will be increasingly irrelevant.

The total quality school's structure may not be a pyramid but rather a disc in which autonomous teams are able to interact with their customers, each other and with the centre. However, the centre only holds as much power as is necessary, authority and responsibility are delegated to teams commensurate with the tasks they have to do. The function of the centre is to provide leadership, to empower and facilitate the teams.

Figure 6.3 shows a quality based organisational structure. This model incorporates a number of features of a quality culture whilst at the same time recognising the accountability of the headteacher. It is not a pseudo-egalitarian approach; rather an attempt to translate theory into practice. The exact designation of the teams will depend on the situation – they may be traditional subject departments or teams responsible for age or ability groupings. The most significant feature is the ability of teams to communicate laterally and their immediacy to their customers, internal and external.

Recruitment and selection

This topic has been chosen as an example because it exemplifies the

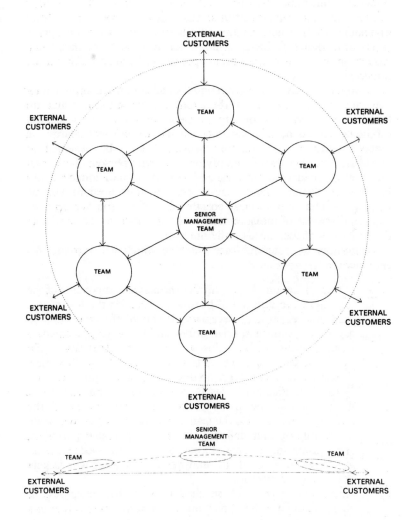

Figure 6.3   A quality based organisational structure

changes that may be necessary to implement a quality culture. It is very easy to caricature selection procedures for teaching posts in schools: application forms that have more space for 'O' levels than for experience; advertisements that invite applications from 'dynamic, exciting and committed teachers looking for an opportunity to work in a challenging and rewarding school' and then being judged on the basis of a restricted application form and a 20 minute interview.

Two factors have to be given equal weighting when approaching the selection process. Firstly the applicants are customers and are therefore entitled to a quality process. Secondly the successful candidate has to be the one that can do the job and shares the school's culture. The selection process has to be designed to maximise the chances of identifying the right person. Too often selection procedures are historic and confirm an individual's ability to do their present job. As far as possible they need to become predictive. This implies clear specification of criteria for appointment and the use of measurement where possible, at the very least the collection of data needs to be objective.

A number of techniques are available which will support this approach:

- Job specification: This identifies the actual components of the job, what the duties will be and so specifies the knowledge skills and experience necessary. It should therefore refer to age range, subject specialisation, ability range and management responsibilities. This is what the school wants the successful candidate to be able to do. (The job specification is developed into an agreed job description after appointment.)
- Person specification: This is the sort of person the school wants and is the most problematic but crucial if the individual is to fit into the team. A lot of work has to be done in identifying and defining the personal qualities that are appropriate to the post. Experience and knowledge are no guarantee of a social 'fit' and yet this is what will largely determine effectiveness.
- Application forms: These need to serve two purposes; to allow candidates the opportunity to describe themselves in a positive way and to allow selectors to make a systematic comparison. Forms should be designed to facilitate these purposes. Letters and CVs are useful but make comparison problematic.
- References: These are useful if information specific to the post is sought, i.e. if the referee is asked to provide evidence

or a judgement on the extent to which the candidate meets the person and job specifications.

- Interviews: The interview has significant potential as a selection process but equally has the greatest opportunities for abuse. In order to avoid subjectivity, bias and dissemination interviews need:

1. agreed and understood criteria;

2. consistent patterns of questioning for each candidate;

3. an agreed means of recording data, e.g. a scoring matrix;

4. trained interviewers;

5. an appropriate setting with suitable facilities for the candidates.

- Analogous testing: Even the most effective interview is limited in its ability to evaluate a candidate's ability to do the job. The use of activities which allow candidates to display skills and qualities appropriate to the post seems essential. In-tray exercises are a common form of this approach but a wide range of others are available. Most importantly the capacity to teach or manage has to be reviewed and hearsay is not sufficient evidence.

- Psychometric testing: This remains a problematic issue but if used in conjunction with a range of techniques has considerable potential to provide objective data to selectors. A wide range of tests are available covering skills and proficiency, aptitude and personality. The use of these tests is contentious, especially in an educational environment which most of them were not designed for. However, they can generate significant comparative data and provide the basis for more informed interviewing.

Accuracy of specification and carefully designed procedures related to the specification will produce data which will inform the final decision.

The selection process also needs to take into account the needs of unsuccessful candidates in providing feedback and advice. As much as anything else recruitment and selection are another component of marketing the school. In the context of reinforcing the culture of a school the selection process must, at least, minimise the chances of an inappropriate appointment. At best it will be a powerful manifestation of a quality culture.

Curriculum planning

The full implications of TQM for the curriculum are properly the subject of a separate study. However, in the context of school management there are some specific issues with regard to the management of the curriculum largely concerned with reconciling customer needs with the deployment of teaching staff, time and resources. The central issue, especially for some secondary schools, is the extent to which the curriculum can be delivered and children's learning managed by one teacher in one classroom teaching one subject for one period to one class. The concept of 'fitness for purpose' raises fundamental questions about the uniformity prescribed by the timetable. There is also the very real issue of trust and delegation. The increasing complexity of the curriculum may also be an imperative for change.

If a team based approach to school structures is adopted then one of the most important elements to be delegated to the team is control of its time. This could imply a timetable that is primarily concerned with shared facilities, e.g. sports hall, science labs, or those in short supply, e.g. technology and music facilities. Otherwise the planning and balance of the delivery of the curriculum would be a matter for the team within the requirements of syllabuses and school procedures. This is an opportunity to reinforce a climate of trust, responsiveness and customer focus. It also empowers the team and helps to create autonomous work teams.

It would be for the team to determine the most appropriate deployment of teaching strategies but the notion of resource based learning has the potential for greater customer satisfaction for children. There is also the significant potential for the creation of management and development time for teachers. This approach requires the implementation of resource based learning, the negotiation of learning contracts and the development of skills in team work, time management and the acceptance of personal responsibility for work rate and completion of tasks. The skills needed for adults to work in a TQM environment are replicated almost exactly in those that children need. The prospects for shared learning and development are significant and exciting. Equally importantly, children will be developing the work skills appropriate to TQM environments in which they might seek employment, which are also relevant to further and higher education.

The creation of team bases also has the potential to enhance the environment and the increased opportunities for sharing between teachers can only enhance professional practice and improve the quality of life. Working with a group of disaffected 15 year old

'Waynes' and 'Traceys' on a Friday afternoon, considering the economic consequences of the Second World War is an experience that needs to be shared with colleagues. There is nothing unique in this approach – it is already found in many primary and special schools and in the art and technology departments of secondary schools. What it does is to try and create a culture where the central purpose of a school – children's learning – can be managed in as consistent a manner as possible so that the culture is made tangible for adults and children and thereby reinforced.

These three examples have tried to demonstrate the relationship between culture, quality and the practical aspects of school management. However it is important to stress that there can be no presecription. The important thing is for schools to understand the implications of quality approaches, identify the appropriate culture and ensure that management structures and processes are consistent with both.

Summary

- An understanding of a school's culture is essential to quality management.
- Culture is the shared understanding of an organisation through rites, ceremonies, language and social interaction.
- There are a range of cultural models – none is right or wrong: the important thing is to understand which is yours.
- A quality culture has a number of specific and unique characteristics.
- Cultures are given expression through structure, focus, communications, style and responsiveness.
- The factors influencing culture are the practical issues of day-to-day management in schools.

Actions

- Understand your school's culture. Is your perception shared by colleagues?
- Is your school's culture given consistent expression through management structures and processes?
- Do your management processes reflect learning processes and vice-versa?
- Review your own behaviour to establish how far it is consistent with leading and managing a quality culture.

7 Leadership

Without appropriate leadership no quality programme will work; only dynamic leadership can create the commitment to drive the strategy. Equally leadership will serve as the most graphic example of what adopting a quality approach actually means in practice. The message is very clear – if there is not total involvement by leadership in quality; if it is not an obsession then forget it! It will not work and may well be counterproductive. The implication of this is that before the issue of quality is raised within the school the quality of leadership may need to be explored.

The purpose of this chapter is to explore the issue of leadership in the context of TQM by examining:

- traditional views of leadership in schools;

- the components of quality leadership.

Traditional views of leadership

Although a caricature, it is probably valid to argue that the primary determinant in selection procedures in education is the capacity of the individual to do her or his existing job. The bulk of the selection process is based on historic data. When the process becomes predictive then it is usually through interview questions, which may or may not be explored in depth and verified by the simplest of procedures. Courses on leadership will usually concentrate on the legal/administrative aspects of leadership; how to run a meeting, how to handle difficult parents, the LEA's administrative procedures. The issue is demonstrated in the research data produced by Hall, Mackay and Morgan (1986) and shown in Figure 7.1.

HEAD	TEACHING	ETHOS	POLICY	OPERATIONS/ ADMIN	HUMAN MANAGEMENT	EXTERNAL
A	14	12	0	25	36	1
B	41	4	3	32	8	12
C	31	12	0	18	27	12
D	0	20	26	19	28	7
E	34	19	1	18	17	1

Figure 7.1 Head's time on task (per cent)

Although this is a limited sample covering a very limited time span it does indicate some highly significant patterns:

- Head 'B' spends 73 per cent of her/his time on teaching and routine matters and only 15 per cent on what would generally be regarded as a leadership function.
- Head 'D' by contrast spends 74 per cent of her/his time on what would be regarded as leadership activities.

Neither head is 'right' or 'wrong' in approach, the important thing is to reflect on the implications of a view of headship which avoids contact with people, as leader, and the implications for the school of limited attention to ethos, policy and personal relationships. It is the purpose of this chapter to argue that the approach to leadership exemplified by head 'B' is inappropriate in the context of total quality management. The difference is between the head as 'doer' and the head as facilitator and enabler. It is equally important to raise the issue of the head's role as leader and her/his relationship with the senior management team.

It is for each individual to decide how far their leadership style is appropriate or inappropriate; the following questions may help clarify the issues:

1. How often do you sit and listen for a whole meeting?
2. Do you have a clear view as to where the school will be in five years' time?
3. How often in the past year have you used the school's aims as the agenda for a meeting or training day?
4. How much time have you spent analysing and discussing your own development needs?

5. How much time do you spend checking the work of others?
6. When did you last listen to pupils talking about their experience of school?
7. How much of your time is spent 'fire fighting'?
8. What proportion of your staff are ready for promotion?
9. What is the perception of your school in the community? How do you know?
10. Does your behaviour put into effect your principles of professional practice?

If the answers to these questions is generally in the negative then the reason advanced will probably be a lack of time. It might be a useful preliminary to implementing a quality programme to create 'quality time' and the first stage in this process is analysis (see Figure 7.2).

The analysis of your results is very much a subjective matter. However, if leading and external relations constitute less than 50 per cent of your actual time then it may be that there is a need for a significant review of your priorities and the way in which you organise your time. Quality management requires explicit leadership, not efficient administration, from the leading professionals. There are numerous self-help manuals available on time management and it is not intended to repeat the advice here. Rather to argue that the components of effective leadership require detailed role analysis and clarification of expectations. So that every individual has a range of responsibilities appropriate to her or his role.

The role of the deputy headteacher is a classic example of ambiguity that inhibits effective leadership. Very often responsibility is delegated but not authority, and this inevitably compromises the ability of individuals to act, requiring duplication of effort and so loss of time. Torrington, Weightman and Johns (1989) summarise this problem:

> The work that deputies did varied enormously both within schools and between schools, but many were personal assistants to the headteacher rather than senior staff with clear and significant responsibilities justifying the status and salary (p.137).

If quality management in schools is to work then it must be perceived as being the responsibility of the senior management team and not one individual – it is too large and complex a job for one person. Equally the effective functioning of the senior management team sends one of the strongest messages about the nature of quality management. (These issues are explored in more depth in Chapter 8.)

On the grid below enter what you believe should be your time allocation for each category. Select a 'typical' day and at five minute intervals not down what you are doing. If possible get someone to track you for the day. Categorise each activity according to the following criteria:

Teaching and supervision: i.e. timetabled lesson or regular break or lunchtime duty.

Administration: low grade, routine, clerical work not needing professional expertise.

Managing: routine meetings, organising, communicating, monitoring, interviewing, delegating, decision making.

External relations: representing the school, dealing with the community.

Leading: planning, creating, empowering, being visible, driving the vision.

No contact: personal time not actually doing the job.

Calculate the percentage of time spent on each activity. Record the results:

	IDEAL ALLOCATION %	ACTUAL %	VARIATION
Teaching			
Administration			
Managing			
External Relations			
Leading			
No contact			

Figure 7.2   Time use analysis

Whilst the role of the headteacher and senior management team is fundamental in terms of leadership, it is not their monopoly. All those who have posts of responsibility also have a commitment to exercise leadership. Thus heads of year and subject are responsible for implementing policy *and* providing leadership for the adults in their team.

The components of quality leadership

The literature on TQM and excellence is quite explicit about the components of leadership. Although there are semantic differences, two issues emerge as being most significant; firstly the importance of distinguishing between leadership and management and, secondly, specifying the appropriate behaviour for leaders.

Much has been written about the relationship between managing and leading. For some writers leadership is a sub-set of management; for others leadership is too intangible a concept to be discussed usefully and the emphasis is therefore on operational issues. This leads to the situation described above by Hall, MacKay and Morgan. HMI have consistently argued that leadership is one of the crucial determinants of an effective school. Schools that are perceived as being less than effective are probably being managed, more or less successfully, rather than being led.

The key differences between leading and managing can be demonstrated in Figure 7.3. This is not to diminish the significance

LEADING is concerned with:	MANAGING is concerned with:
VISION	IMPLEMENTATION
STRATEGIC ISSUES	OPERATIONAL ISSUES
TRANSFORMATION	TRANSACTION
ENDS	MEANS
PEOPLE	SYSTEMS
DOING THE RIGHT THINGS	DOING THINGS RIGHT

Figure 7.3   Leading and managing

of managing; it is a crucial determinant of organisational success but it has to operate within a context and according to explicit criteria and it is the function of leadership to provide the context and criteria. Senior management teams thus need to be concerned with values, direction, the long term and crucially, enabling others to fulfil the central purpose of the school.

In order to achieve this, it is proposed that there are five key components to leadership in a quality environment:

- vision;
- creativity;
- sensitivity;
- empowering;
- managing change.

These components are not offered as a hierarchy, indeed they are highly interdependent and each presupposes the others to be fully effective.

Vision

Much that has been discussed in Chapter 5 applies to this section. However, the emphasis here is on the shared vision of headteacher and senior management. Somewhere in the job descriptions of headteacher and senior staff, and in the published functions of the senior management, there needs to be a reference to the responsibility for generating and driving the school's vision. This will involve consultation and communication but it should be seen as a fundamental task without which all other activity will be at best reactive, at worst peripheral and random.

The purpose of vision is to help the school move from the known to the unknown; to set out the hopes and aspirations of the school for children, community and staff. Crucially the vision articulates and defines the values of the school, making them real and attainable. The vision has to be expressed in images, metaphors and models so as to organise meaning for all those involved in working in the school. The well articulated vision helps to answer the questions 'Why are we doing this?', 'What should we be doing?' and 'How should we be doing it?'

The clarity and practicality of a senior management team's vision will do much to determine the success or failure of a school. The decisions relating to pupils' learning, community involvement, decision making and the development of teachers will have a significant impact on the standing of the school in the community.

The senior management team that has a clear vision is characterised by:

- constant reference to the vision in action;
- frequent recognition of future challenges;
- constant contact with all members of the school community;
- openness to ideas;
- recognition and celebration of strengths and successes.

The senior management team that lacks vision will be primarily concerned with:

- routine decision making and problem solving;
- bureaucratic relationships;
- 'distant' personal relationships;

- constant stress on failure and weakness;
- reinforcing the status-quo.

A vision needs to reconcile a wide range of factors in order to provide the basis for empowering leadership.

1. It needs to focus on the moral and aesthetic dimensions of work; it must give expression to what is perceived as good and beautiful – the ideal that is aspired to. Education, as few other social activities, lends itself to the expression of such values.
2. The vision must be challenging and inspiring and act as a focus for motivation; it must articulate an ideal which challenges the mundane and rejects conservation of the norm simply because it is the norm.
3. The vision must reinforce success and celebrate strengths – paradoxically it must consolidate that which is valid and be capable of responding to a changing environment at the same time.
4. The vision should talk in terms of ideals and principles and yet be capable of being translated into specific action. Above all the vision must be capable of being communicated, and becoming meaningful, to everyone to whom it applies. This means children, parents, non-teaching staff, governors and the wider community as well as teachers. It should be possible to identify concrete steps towards attaining the vision.

The process of actually articulating the vision requires high level reflection and introspection – the outcomes of this meditation need to be shared, tested and refined and, crucially, responses listened to. The questions in Figure 7.4 might help clarify the issues.

Creativity

It is frequently stated that the Education Reform Act has challenged all existing assumptions about the management of schools. If this is the case, and there is little reason to doubt it, then reliance on traditional approaches to management are inappropriate. Indeed the use of traditional techniques and solutions may be counter productive if not actually detrimental. One of the principal factors in headteachers taking early retirement has been a natural reluctance to abandon established methods of working. However unique problems require unique solutions. Creativity, the generation of

---

1. If my child were a pupil at this school, what would I expect for her/him?

2. What are the major externally imposed challenges that we will have to meet?

3. What do our clients really want?

4. What are our most significant skills and capabilities?

5. In what ways are we unique?

6. What is our potential as a school?

7. What are our most significant successes?

8. What problems do we need to overcome?

9. What can we learn from other schools?

10. How will we know that we are getting it right?

11. Looking back over the past five years, what would I change?

12. What single thing must we get right?

Figure 7.4   Evolving the vision

imaginative and radical solutions to apparently intractable problems, thus becomes an essential component of leadership.

However it is again important to stress that this function, although a highly desirable individual trait, is substantially enhanced through a team approach. No amount of dedicated reading of management 'self-improvement' manuals will bring about flashes of creativity. Working in teams, on the other hand, can release creative power. These issues will be explored in more depth in Chapter 8. It is worth stressing that the sum of the parts is greater than the whole and that it has been consistently demonstrated that teams are more creative, more likely to generate radical alternatives and are better placed to review and evaluate possible solutions. At the same time individuals do need to generate solutions and creative thinking is a skill that can be developed. The characteristics of the creative thinker include the following:

1. Being at ease with complexity.
2. Being relaxed with abstract concepts.

3. Using a variety of problem solving approaches.
4. Synthesising rather than describing data.
5. Persisting with an apparently intractable issue.
6. Not being afraid of being wrong.
7. Displaying naïveté in questioning.
8. Accepting all possible solutions, however apparently ridiculous.
9. Accepting possible solutions from any source.
10. Visualising all possible viewpoints.
11. Organising data in a variety of permutations.
12. Being aware of a range of sources for solutions through reading and networking.

Many of these characteristics are to be found in the notion of 'helicoptering'; the ability of an individual to rise above the minutiae of a situation, to place it in context, identify the best solution and then descend with a clear view of what needs to happen. Flying the helicopter helps to identify the wood and the trees, to note the paths and the clearings and to avoid blundering around in circles in the undergrowth convinced that working hard is a substitute for solving the problem. A number of problem solving techniques are identified in Chapter 4 but they are largely for use in groups; the following are suggested individual strategies.

Self-analysis
What kind of thinker are you? What are your values? What are your 'hidden agendas'? The answers to these questions are a fundamental precursor to developing creative approaches. A person's intellectual history, e.g. their academic training may well determine the extent to which they are conservationist or creative. The level of personal security will influence the level of change that can be tolerated, the openness to new ideas. The process of self-analysis may lead to the decision to make better use of the skills of colleagues, to change working practices or to seek training.

Targeting
This technique involves selecting a very specific issue or process and generating as many new ways of approaching it as possible. The topic might be very mundane – litter in school; or very complex – improving communication with parents. The technique is to write down a new way of approaching it which describes what will actually happen, i.e. the strategy must be expressed in terms of action. This technique works best if 'anything goes', all ideas are worth considering.

Challenging

This approach involves questioning the status-quo; asking, 'What if?' questions. Reflecting on what would happen if established roles and procedures were broken, generating alternatives to the established work patterns. 'Why does X always do this? What will happen if it is not done? What will happen if somebody else does it?'

Thinking skills

It may be worth considering that creativity and generating ideas are skills that need developing like any others. The works of Edward De Bono and Tony Buzanare may be worth exploring.

Transferring

This process involves speculating on alternative scenarios. It might involve reflection on how other cultures, institutions, historical or contemporary figures might respond to the situation. This approach can also be parasitic; taking an idea from a course or conference or reading and speculating on its applicability. Creativity often consists of reordering or rearranging existing ideas to suit a particular situation.

Quality thinking

This is the most complex and intangible approach – it could be described as reflection or even meditation. The process has five components:

- Recognising the years of experience, understanding and intuition and letting them become a resource.
- Synthesising that experience by a process of reflection and ordering.
- Explaining all the facets of understanding by focusing very precisely on all the constituents of an issue.
- Drawing on the intuition to enhance appreciation and awareness.
- Formulating responses based on the improved awareness.

This activity may be significantly improved by training in meditation techniques or it may be 30 minutes in the day for undisturbed thinking. In schools there is a desperate need for leaders to have thinking time. It is usually lost, swamped by day-to-day demands. These demands are real and important but the issue is:

'What are the implications of leaders not thinking'?

Sensitivity

There are three concerns in the area of interpersonal skills for leadership; firstly the quality of personal relationships will often be a prime determinant of client satisfaction, secondly there is a need for consistency in all processes, and thirdly the behaviour of leaders is a crucial model in the implementation of a quality programme. In schools, where social relationships are the fundamental and most significant process, it is difficult to overemphasise the centrality of high level personal skills. The behaviour of leaders will be a key determinant in motivation, creating a culture and in forming the reactions of those with whom leaders come into contact.

For these reasons sensitivity has been chosen as a key characteristic – sensitivity in relationships with others but also sensitivity in personal awareness of the impact made on others. The major problem is that personality cannot be legislated for: no series of prescriptions will change inappropriate behaviour (possibly quite the reverse) so self awareness is a crucial component of developing sensitivity. There are many courses offered in the area of interpersonal skills so it is not appropriate to offer diagnostic activities in the context of this book but rather to propose an inventory of relevant skills and behaviour. It is suggested that the following characteristics are particularly relevant:

- listening;
- giving feedback;
- negotiating;
- giving praise;
- managing conflict;
- networking;
- empathising.

Isolating these characteristics in this way might create a false impression – in fact they are highly interdependent and each presupposes the others if it is to be practised successfully. The desired outcome is best exemplified in the notion of 'win–win'. This describes one of the four possible outcomes from any transaction: these may be summarised as in Figure 7.5.

There is clearly one desirable outcome – that we both win. The other variants all imply defeat for one or both parties and this can only serve to diminish both, to exacerbate personal relationships and

We win	I win you lose
I lose you win	We lose

Figure 7.5 Winning and losing

compromise self-esteem. Win–win does not imply compromise or dilution but rather sophisticated skills which build on a foundation of respect. Win–win situations are most likely to result when:

- all desired outcomes are expressed;
- commonality is sought and emphasised;
- the emphasis is on the problem, not the person;
- alternative solutions are proposed;
- the emphasis is on process and outcome;
- the implications of both losing are recognised.

In order to achieve the situation of 'we' rather than 'me' the skills identified below are all relevant and have to be incorporated into the criteria for appropriate behaviour.

Listening

Most people can hear perfectly adequately but a minority can actually listen in the sense of genuinely attending. Active listening, i.e. total involvement is difficult but vitally important as it demonstrates commitment and involvement and ensures that information is gathered and correctly received. Listening is as much about the unspoken as the spoken, it is about sensitivity to feelings and perceptions. Active listening requires:

- eye contact at regular intervals;
- body language which is supportive and reinforcing, e.g. attentive body posture, nods and smiles, reinforcing hand gestures, nods and positive sounds;
- providing regular feedback;

- using reinforcing questioning styles to corroborate and confirm;
- avoiding negative behaviour, e.g. being distracted, fidgeting or allowing interruptions.

Giving feedback

Feedback is a demanding but highly significant skill, it involves reiterating to the speaker what she/he has just said. It checks the accuracy of listening, allows confirmation of feelings and reinforces the significance attached to what has been articulated. In essence the listener 'plays back' what has been said but also checks interpretation. Feedback works best when:

- it is non-judgemental;
- it uses the same language;
- feelings and perceptions are confirmed;
- the information given is built on;
- it is specific to the individual;
- agreed criteria are employed.

However, feedback serves another, fundamentally important function in that it demonstrates the respect, seriousness and commitment of the listener.

Negotiating

Negotiating skills are concerned with reaching an outcome, a decision taken, a problem solved and, at the same time, improving personal relationships and enhancing mutual esteem. In order for this to happen a number of very specific skills and behaviours are necessary:

- focus on the issue not the person;
- build on proposals 'yes, and...' not 'yes, but...';
- obtain and agree facts;
- explain and justify differences;
- articulate feelings;
- use the full range of questioning styles;
- summarise and feedback;
- generate mutually agreed alternatives.

Giving praise

This is one of the most neglected areas of leadership in schools.

Teachers who are consistent in their belief in the importance of praising children consistently fail to recognise each other. Praise implies recognition, celebration and reinforcement; fundamental needs of all adults as well as children. However there is a need to avoid gratuitous and superficial responses. Genuine praise has the following characteristics:

- It is specific to an individual.
- It refers to a specific event.
- It gives reasons.
- It is unconditional.
- It is not linked to an ulterior motive.
- It is given at the time, on the spot.

Managing conflict

Conflict in organisations is almost inevitable and indeed, if properly managed, can be a powerful stimulus to action, creativity and the resolution of hidden tensions. Managing conflict means that it is not avoided nor 'glossed-over' but rather dealt with directly and explicitly. Positive conflict management involves:

- openly recognising that there is a conflict;
- understanding the motives at work;
- depersonalising the issue;
- empathising with the other person;
- avoiding prescriptive statements;
- generating alternative solutions;
- continuous feedback to confirm understanding;
- accepting incremental solutions;
- agreeing monitoring procedures to ensure implementation.

Networking

Networking is the process of establishing and maintaining a series of co-operative relationships that help get things done. Successful leaders have the ability to identify who can help, i.e. who has the knowledge, access or skills and the ability to mobilise that help. Active networking involves nurturing contacts, reciprocating support and identifying those who need to be cultivated. One of the most important indicators of an effective team is the strength of the network characterised by:

- effectiveness of communications;
- importance attached to regular contact;

- time for regular contact;
- offers of reciprocal support;
- use of the network to facilitate specific agendas;
- clear identification of who can help to get things done.

Empathising

This is the ability to understand how things seem to another person; to be able to appreciate the significance, value and relevance attached to a given situation. Any form of communication is likely to be compromised unless there is a willingness to accept that subjectivity defines reality. Obtaining real understanding involves:

- active listening;
- checking through feedback;
- understanding 'why?' as well as 'what?';
- demonstrating recognition of the situation;
- challenging to clarify;
- talking about one's own experience;
- visualising the situation.

Sensitivity is thus about caring, respecting and cherishing. It only has meaning when it is expressed in action and this means:

- creating winning situations;
- listening first;
- understanding;
- collaborative problem solving;
- emphasising process issues;
- awareness of others.

Empowering

Empowering is a fundamental component of quality leadership; in essence it involves releasing the potential of individuals – allowing them to flourish and grow, to release their capacity for infinite improvement. In many ways the whole of this book is about empowerment, in that it involves providing direction (Chapters 5 and 7), working through teams (Chapter 8), creating appropriate structures and processes (Chapters 4 and 6) and emphasising the importance of personal relationships (Chapter 7). This section will therefore concentrate on one specific issue which is very much at the behest of individual leaders – involvement through delegation.

Schools are bizarre institutions when it comes to delegation – on the one hand they delegate awesome levels of responsibility and authority, i.e. to the classroom teacher who will have a high degree of personal autonomy, but on the other hand they are unable to replicate this when it comes to management. Torrington, Weightman and Johns (1989) provide a number of examples of this failure to delegate (pp. 150–161, 167–169). The failure to delegate inevitably implies a limitation on involvement and thereby a lack of trust.

Real delegation has a number of significant benefits:

- It is a real and direct demonstration of trust; it translates the rhetoric of trust into a tangible expression.
- It is one of the most powerful means of facilitating development, it allows real learning to take place – by doing the job.
- It forces a radical evaluation of the key purpose of a job and questions those aspects which may be enjoyable or therapeutic but are best delegated.
- It creates the time to lead by delegating the management and administrative tasks that are more appropriately done by somebody else.

Delegation is a balancing act between a number of variables; accountability, control, authority, responsibility and training. Accountability cannot be delegated as that would amount to abdication, which is totally inappropriate. Therefore a measure of control has to be retained. However, control can be through setting and reviewing targets as much as constant reporting and checking. Delegation without authority is unfair and unworkable, it is not true delegation as it implies constant referring back – which defeats the object of the exercise! If authority is delegated then so is responsibility, as a degree of personal autonomy is then established. Responsibility without authority is cruel and a recipe for failure. If both are effectively delegated then ownership is created; the job becomes a real one rather than the 'dumping of chores'.

Any leader or manager who states that they are unable to delegate because 'the staff aren't up to it' – 'they are bound to mess it up' – is condemning himself or herself rather than the staff. If staff have not been trained and developed then that is the responsibility of the manager, not the employee's. As part of the delegation process, training needs have to be identified at the outset in order to ensure that motivation is matched by capability. The components of delegation are shown in Figure 7.6.

Unless there is full autonomy in all components of the job, delegation will not work. The delegator will not have 'let go' and the

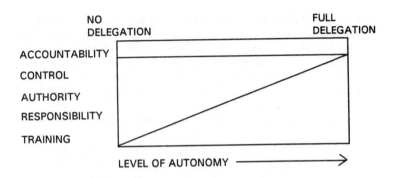

Figure 7.6   The delegation process

delegatee will not feel fully trusted. If the other components of quality management are in place then delegation is not only 'no-risk' but is actually seen as a normal way of working. As with so many aspects of TQM, models already exist in schools – in the effective classroom:

- the underlying purpose is clear, understood and accepted;
- clear targets are negotiated and agreed;
- the timescale is established;
- criteria for acceptable performance are clear;
- outcomes and check-points are defined.

If these structural issues are clear then the next stage is for the delegator to adopt appropriate behaviour:

- the delegatee initiates contacts – not the delegator;
- responsibility is publicly located with the delegatee – and this is reflected in private; there is constant reinforcement;
- requests for information and decisions are referred to the delegatee;
- questions are met with questions, not prescriptions;
- requests for resources are met on merit, not seen as signs of failure.

Delegation empowers because it has the potential to demonstrate trust, create real, purposeful, jobs and, crucially provide a vehicle for self-actualisation, esteem and achievement. Managing children's learning is all about these factors. It is strange that what happens in the classroom is not always mirrored in the staffroom.

In order to make delegation work the following stages might be followed:

1. Is your job description up-to-date and accurate? Does it reflect the key purpose of your job?
2. Does the reality of your working life reflect your job purpose? (use the time – use analysis Figure 7.2).
3. On the basis of this analysis identify those parts of your job:
    (a) which only you have the skills, knowledge and experience for;
    (b) which are unique to your seniority and responsibility;
    (c) which are routine and standardised;
    (d) which consume a disproportionate part of your time;
    (e) which do not require your skills, knowledge and experience.

4. Which members of your staff are ready for promotion, development, in need of change, ready for redeployment?
5. Use the appraisal process to identify and reconcile school needs, individual needs, opportunities for development.
6. Identify training needs, train and let go!

In essence empowerment is about seeing people as being capable of infinite improvement and development. Organisations exist to enhance people, not to stultify them. Every leader has to recognise that every single employee is a customer, entitled to quality in all aspects of their lives.

Managing change

The leader has to love change, to be excited by it and to welcome it and at the same time create the environment that allows objectives to be met and tasks to be completed. The management of complex change in schools does not require the heroic warrior leader (Attila or Boadicea the head), instead it requires the facilitator of learning. For, as Fullan (1985) has argued, change is about learning – it is an internal process which has to focus on behaviour and attitudes more than resources. Managers in schools are already experts in managing change; they manage the most complex transitional process of all, the education of children. Compared to the transformation that takes place in the infant school, the harnessing of energy in the junior years and the complexity of the secondary school the demands of the Education Reform Act are relatively minor.

Leadership in the context of change is about facilitating learning, allowing people to change rather than reacting to change. In order to achieve this, a range of knowledge, skills and behavioural characteristics are required in leaders. These are outlined in Figure 7.7.

KNOWLEDGE	SKILLS	BEHAVIOUR
INDIVIDUAL MOTIVATION	LISTENING EMPATHISING	CONSTANT REFERENCE TO THE VISION VALUES PEOPLE – AND SHOWS IT
ORGANISATIONS AS SOCIAL SYSTEMS	GIVING FEEDBACK QUESTIONING	BREAKS BUREAUCRACY REINFORCEMENT OF SUCCESS
THE SCHOOL'S ENVIRONMENT	TARGET SETTING	WORKS ON FACTS LEADS BY EXAMPLE
MANAGEMENT PROCESSES	CONFLICT MANAGEMENT MANAGING LEARNING	OBSESSED WITH CUSTOMER SATISFACTION
CHANGE PROCESSES	ANALYSING & SYNTHESIZING	TOLERANCE OF AMBIGUITY
LEARNING STYLES	CREATIVITY	OPTIMISTIC OUTLOOK
CUSTOMER REQUIREMENTS	PROBLEM SOLVING	ACCEPTING OF FAILURE
DEVELOPMENT STRATEGIES	COUNSELLING DELEGATING COMMUNICATING	LOW ESTEEM NEEDS CELEBRATION OF WORK AS FUN ALWAYS AVAILABLE OPENNESS PROVIDES A MODEL

Figure 7.7   The components of leadership for managing change (derived from Everard and Morris 1990 and Peters 1988)

It is not by chance that there are far more references to behaviour than to knowledge and that many of the skills simply enhance the capacity to behave in a certain way. The concept of managing change implies a package of knowledge and skills that can be deployed. In fact the most powerful factor is the action taken by a leader. Change is managed through behaviour not accumulated knowledge or unapplied skills.

One of the most potent images of the twentieth century is that of the wagon train in the Hollywood western. The wagons progress serenely across the prairie following the trail blazed by the leader (who is usually motionless on a hilltop highlighted by a convenient sunset). She has delegated responsibility to outriders to manage the actual progress of the wagons, to work out the precise route, to mend broken wheels and to circle the wagons when danger threatens. At the back of the wagon train is the chuck wagon (crewed by an irascible old man and a youth with an unfortunate tendency to break into song). The wagon train will quickly fall apart, lose its way and its purpose if the leader spends her time in the wagon counting the beans, worrying about the bacon and measuring out the coffee. She brings about change by being in front.

Leadership and change are synonymous, no leader has ever been regarded as great because of her or his ability to sustain the status-quo. Leadership is about personal change and organisational growth. In the context of total quality management the primary responsibility of leadership is to create the environment in which continuous improvement can take place. Leadership is about the sunset, not the beans.

Summary

- Traditional approaches to headship may not be appropriate in the context of TQM.
- Leading and managing need to be carefully distinguished.
- Self-analysis is an essential pre-requisite to effective leadership.
- Leadership is not the monopoly of the head.
- Vision is the driving force for leadership.
- Creative problem solving is an essential characteristic.
- Sensitivity in terms of personal relationships is a fundamental requirement.
- Leadership is empowering others.
- Leadership is about changing.

Action

- Find out how your leadership style is regarded by your colleagues.
- Use the appraisal process to review your personal effectiveness.
- Analyse your use of time – how much leadership time are you losing by doing the mundane and routine (however satisfying)?
- Are the deputies in your school leaders or clerks?
- Identify a leader whom you admire, spend time shadowing her/him and set up a mentoring arrangement.
- Invest in two days' team thinking time (a weekend in a good hotel can cost less than a day's supply). Use a consultant to facilitate the process.
- Use the appraisal process to empower your colleagues.

- Explore the opportunities for leadership and team development training.
- In the next senior appointment you are involved in, identify detailed criteria for leadership characteristics and the means to assess them.

8 Teams

A team is a quality group. Almost all organisations and schools in particular create teams as the major vehicle for organising work. However, there is a substantial gap between labelling a group a team and creating an effective work team which is able to function in a total quality environment. Too often teams are established and expected to operate simply by virtue of having delegated tasks – little consideration is given to the way in which the team functions. Designing and developing teams is rarely seen as a priority in schools – they are created by virtue of knowledge, experience and status – not by the ability of the individuals to work collaboratively. The purpose of this chapter is to examine:

- the characteristics of effective teams;
- team building;
- team development;
- quality circles.

Teams do make a difference – there are abundant analogies to be drawn from sporting activities but they can all be summarised by considering the relationship between sporting expertise and skill, leadership and team success. Technical skill does not guarantee success, the expert practitioner is not necessarily the best captain and assembling the most talented individuals does not always create a winning team. Just as expertise with the cricket bat is not necessarily indicative of leadership skills, so expertise in the classroom is no guarantee of the ability to collaborate with colleagues. There can be a real tension between the autonomy (and isolation) of the classroom and the need to work in a team. This view is reflected in the work of Murgatroyd (1985) and Torrington,

Weightman and Johns (1989); synthesising their views produces the following analysis of the problematic nature of teams in schools:

1. School 'teams' place great emphasis on the tasks (agendas) of managing and little emphasis on the processes (networks). 'Getting the job done' is seen as more significant than how the job is done. However, the lack of concern with process can often be to the detriment of task achievement.
2. 'Teams' in schools lack a 'bias for action' – they spend too much time debating issues and principles (over which they may have little or no control) and too little time solving problems, formulating solutions and developing a commitment to action. Groups debate – teams act.
3. Poorly managed 'teams' in schools are reactive – responding to events rather than anticipating them and often seeking solace in routine chores rather than driving the vision and becoming anticipatory. This leads to work becoming a chore and ritualistic.
4. 'Teams' are often not concerned with their own social needs – they spend insufficient time recognising, reinforcing and celebrating each other. Equally they will not devote time to planning and reviewing their work nor will they seek to develop their skills as a team or the potential of individuals to become effective team members.

The working routines of these 'immature' teams will often be characterised by very formal social exchanges (e.g. the use of titles rather than first names); the use of quasi-parliamentary procedures (e.g. 'On a point of information, headmistress, may I enquire through the chair...?'); the reading of documents to the team and the active pursuit of red herrings (e.g. debating the influence of social hierarchies of 19th Century England when planning the seating arrangement for prize giving).

The characteristics of effective teams

A synthesis of the research of McGregor (1960), Likert (1961) and Blake and Mouton (1964) produces the 'map' of effective team functioning shown in Figure 8.1.

The strength and creative potential of teams is derived from the application of each of these characteristics, but more importantly from the critical mass achieved when they are linked and synergy is achieved. At that point the 'whole' is considerably greater than the sum of the parts. Each characteristic is complex and demanding in

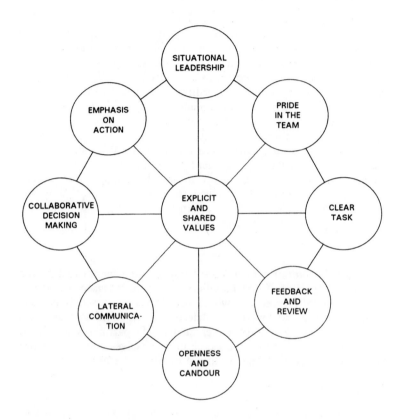

Figure 8.1   The components of effective team work

its own right and needs to be explored in some detail.

1.   Explicit and shared values

This issue has already been explored in Chapters 5 and 7. However, it is worth stressing that no team can operate effectively unless it is working in a context where the values are clear and agreed and translated into a mission. Equally it is important that the personal values of team members are public and understood. Everyone knows the values that everyone else brings to the team so they are not being continually debated (see 'forming' and 'storming' below).

2. *Situational leadership*

The principles that were discussed in Chapter 7 are particularly relevant here, Effective teams require leadership that displays all the characteristics explored previously. However, in the context of team working a new dimension is necessary – the willingness and ability of the designated leader to defer, to stand back and allow other team members to assume control according to the needs of the situation. This implies a detailed understanding of the knowledge and capabilities of each team member and the 'grace' to pass on authority. For example a deputy headteacher may have highly sophisticated decision making and interpersonal skills and so is the best person to chair management meetings. A relatively junior member of staff may be the most knowledgeable about flexible learning – she should be allowed to lead and is entitled to the wholehearted support of the team. In this way the team is effective and a team member is empowered.

3. *Pride in the team*

This implies commitment and involvement and is manifested in high morale and loyalty. Team members believe in themselves, in each other and in the team as a whole and this is expressed frequently both internally and externally. There is a self-fulfilling belief that 'We are good and we can deliver quality'. Departments in schools that are doing well and feel good about themselves quickly transmit this. There is even the possibility of displays of enthusiasm!

4. *Clear task*

Without a clear task effective team-work is impossible. Teams that are set intangible goals, unclear outcomes and lack information and resources and a time-scale are unlikely to be motivated; in fact they are more likely to plod and amble rather than sprint. For a team to sprint it requires:

- specific outcomes;
- performance indicators;
- realistic targets;
- information and resources;
- nurturing and reinforcing;
- time-scale.

Sprint teams have their eyes clearly on the tape, know exactly how far they have to travel and explode into action. Too often in school teams are sent on country rambles when they need to be racing. To switch the sporting metaphor (somewhat abruptly) teams do not win by debating if the goal posts are moving – they win by scoring goals.

5. Feedback and review

Effective teams are very self-conscious; they devote time to getting feedback from their clients and from each other. Team review is a permanent feature of every activity. This is not introspection for its own sake but rather review as part of a learning process. The review of task completion *and* team processes provides the basis for change through learning. Sophisticated teams will abandon the task to explore what is happening in process teams – to identify and reinforce success and to tackle problems until they are solved. The team that does not invest in itself is unlikely to add value to its way of working (see Chapter 4 for review techniques).

6. Openness and candour

All issues are open to discussion, there are no 'hidden agendas' and every member of the team feels able to offer suggestions, ideas, comments, information, praise and criticism. Relationships are comfortable and relaxed – the climate is supportive; 'Yes and...' is used more than 'Yes but...'. Criticism is frank and direct and directed towards the problem not the person. Criticism is not negative but is used to remove an obstacle. Team members express their feelings as well as their opinions on the task; the effective team cultivates the ability to talk easily about emotional and personal responses.

7. Lateral communication

Effective teams are also characterised by lateral communication; team members are able to communicate with each other without reference to the team leader or other members of the team. Complex networks are formed and nourished by the team – they are not seen as a threat but rather as potential enrichment. Equally sub-sets within the team are open and report back. This process in itself develops skills and reinforces relationships to the benefit of the team as a whole.

8. Collaborative decision making

Effective teams make the best decisions – the decision is the 'best fit' and will be fully implemented by team members. Quality decisions emerge from the full utilisation of the knowledge and skills of team members, which means that the decision will have been made in the minimum time but to maximum effect. Collaborative decision making avoids voting, alternative viewpoints are worked through and disagreements resolved. Crucially the team is enhanced socially by the decision making process.

9.   *Emphasis on action*

Teams make things happen – their decisions are expressed in terms of action. Each team member knows what has to be done, by whom and when? Effective teams do not write minutes of their meetings – they issue agreed actions.

Effective teams expect to accomplish the impossible – miracles may take a little longer. Teams balance task and process – what the job is and how it is done, see Figure 8.2 Position 'A' represents an

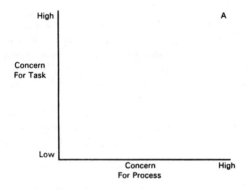

Position 'A' is the optimum for team effectiveness.

Figure 8.2   Task and process (after Blake and Mouton 1978)

ideal, the optimum to be worked for where the task is achieved efficiently and effectively and there are high level personal relationships – quality is delivered in terms of product and process. Any other position on the grid compromises one or both. High concern for tasks with little regard for process denies the social significance of work, high concern for process at the expense of task removes the point of the team's existence. The design, recruitment and development of the team will have a significant impact on its outcomes both in terms of task and process.

Team building

Effective teams do not happen by chance, they have to be deliberately created and systematically managed. Given the significance of the outcomes of educational decision making and the pressures on the time of teachers and managers in schools the importance of creating effective teams cannot be overstated. Teams in schools are rarely created with principles of team building in mind. Team membership is often a low order selection factor if it is an issue at all. Induction is likely to be in terms of administrative procedures if it takes place.

It may be appropriate to distinguish between structural and ad hoc teams in schools. Structural teams will include the senior management team, academic and pastoral units and groups set up to manage specific issues such as the curriculum, budget or staff development. Ad hoc groups are set up to manage specific issues, e.g. cross-curricular initiatives, implementation of a particular reform or event. In both cases the capability of teachers to work as leader or member of a team will not be an issue. Membership will be on the basis of experience, status or volunteering. Significance might be attached to consultation; rarely will the capabilities of the person as a team member be a factor. This might help to explain the frustration that is often experienced by so-called team members in schools – the frustration arises because they cannot function as members of teams. Figure 8.3 provides a starting point for analysing team effectiveness.

A score in excess of 35 indicates that the rest of this chapter is probably redundant. 25–35 indicates there will probably be something of interest for you; 9–24 – I just hope this chapter can meet your needs! Once you have completed this analysis get other members of your team to complete it independently. Then use a team meeting to discuss your perceptions by displaying the scores on a flip-chart or OHP and analysing the significance of any discrepancies in perceptions. (If your score is below 20–25 it will probably be very difficult to get this review on the agenda!)

Another means of analysing the maturity of the team is to consider its level of development. Tuckman (1985) suggests that teams go through a series of clear stages in the move to effectiveness, illustrated in Figure 8.4.

The central principle in team building is to minimise the time spent forming and storming, to make norming as powerful as possible and to devote the maximum amount of time to performing. It is not possible to 'short-circuit' the process, i.e. avoid forming and storming, but with deliberate team management the negative aspects

Complete this analysis thinking of a team of which you are currently a member. Score each
section according to how you perceived the applicability of each set of statements.

1.	Values and purpose are not discussed	1	2	3	4	5	We share and implement common values
2.	Leadership is restricted to one or two people	1	2	3	4	5	Leadership is shared according to need
3.	Team membership is a chore and a bore	1	2	3	4	5	There is genuine pride in team leadership
4.	Objectives are not shared or understood	1	2	3	4	5	We are committed to our objectives
5.	We never talk about how we are doing	1	2	3	4	5	We systematically review our performance
6.	Communication is restricted, cautious	1	2	3	4	5	Communication is open, robust, honest.
7.	The team leader dominates	1	2	3	4	5	Our abilities are fully utilised, we are trusted
8.	Decisions are taken by voting or by the leader	1	2	3	4	5	We all share and support decisions
9.	Action is unclear or absent	1	2	3	4	5	We all know who does what by when.

Figure 8.3   Team effectiveness analysis

can be minimised. Analysis of the way in which some teams operate
would suggest that they never get beyond the first two stages, all
their time being spent in debating the task and sorting out personal
relationships. Eventually they have to accept an imposed decision
and are unable to produce acceptable conclusions in the time
available. There are a number of possible explanations for this:

1. The task itself is impossible – it has not been properly
    defined or is beyond the resources of the team, i.e. it is
    inappropriate.
2. The team has not been designed to accomplish the task, i.e.
    the wrong people have been nominated or allowed to
    volunteer.
3. The team lacks the skills to work together.

The first problem can only be resolved by appropriate delegation
(see Chapter 7); the second issue is dealt with below and the third in
the next section in this chapter – team development.
    If teams are to move rapidly from forming to performing then the

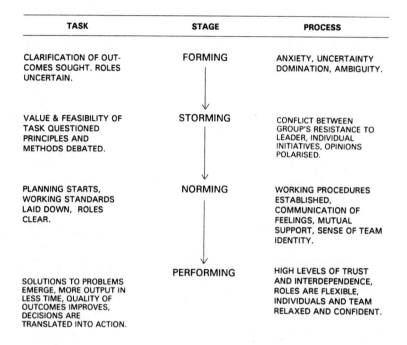

TASK	STAGE	PROCESS
CLARIFICATION OF OUT-COMES SOUGHT. ROLES UNCERTAIN.	FORMING	ANXIETY, UNCERTAINTY DOMINATION, AMBIGUITY.
VALUE & FEASIBILITY OF TASK QUESTIONED PRINCIPLES AND METHODS DEBATED.	STORMING	CONFLICT BETWEEN GROUP'S RESISTANCE TO LEADER, INDIVIDUAL INITIATIVES, OPINIONS POLARISED.
PLANNING STARTS, WORKING STANDARDS LAID DOWN, ROLES CLEAR.	NORMING	WORKING PROCEDURES ESTABLISHED, COMMUNICATION OF FEELINGS, MUTUAL SUPPORT, SENSE OF TEAM IDENTITY.
SOLUTIONS TO PROBLEMS EMERGE, MORE OUTPUT IN LESS TIME, QUALITY OF OUTCOMES IMPROVES, DECISIONS ARE TRANSLATED INTO ACTION.	PERFORMING	HIGH LEVELS OF TRUST AND INTERDEPENDENCE, ROLES ARE FLEXIBLE, INDIVIDUALS AND TEAM RELAXED AND CONFIDENT.

Figure 8.4   Stages in team maturity

capabilities of team members to work in a team need to be a significant element in team design and recruitment. Some of the most important work in this respect has been done by Belbin (1981). Belbin analysed the performance of management teams and found that there was not always a correlation between a team's ability to perform and the intellectual qualities and experience of its members. In fact the so-called 'alpha' teams – the brightest and best – were often out-performed by apparently random groupings. In analysing the reasons for this Belbin concluded that the behaviour of individuals in teams is at least, if not more, significant a factor than ability or experience. Teams are social entities and their performance will be determined by social interactions and these, according to Belbin, can be identified and analysed.

Belbin postulates eight team roles; these are outlined in Figure 8.5.

TYPE	CHARACTERISTICS	POSITIVE QUALITIES	ALLOWABLE WEAKNESSES
COMPANY WORKER	TRANSLATES IDEAS INTO PRACTICE, GETS ON WITH THE JOB, WORKS WITH CARE & THOROUGHNESS.	ORGANISING ABILITY, COMMON SENSE, INTEGRITY, HARD WORKING, SELF DISCIPLINED, LOYAL.	LACK OF FLEXIBILITY AND ADAPTABILITY.
CHAIR	CONTROLS & COORDINATES, DRIVEN BY OBJECTIVES, UTILISES TEAM RESOURCES.	ENTHUSIASTIC, ASSERTIVE, FLEXIBLE, STRONG SENSE OF DUTY.	NOT REALLY CREATIVE OR INSPIRATIONAL.
SHAPER	PUSHES TO GET THE JOB DONE, INSPIRES, MAKES THINGS HAPPEN.	DRIVE, ENTHUSIASM, CHALLENGES ROLES, COMMANDS RESPECT, INTOLERANT OF VAGUENESS.	NEEDS TO BE IN CHARGE, IMPULSIVE, IMPATIENT, UNDULY SENSITIVE TO CRITICISM.
INNOVATOR	ADVANCES NEW IDEAS, SYNTHESISES KNOWLEDGE.	INTELLIGENCE, IMAGINATION, CREATIVITY UNORTHODOX.	PREFERS IDEAS TO PEOPLE, IGNORES PRACTICAL ISSUES.
RESOURCE INVESTIGATOR	IDENTIFIES IDEAS AND RESOURCES FROM OUTSIDE THE TEAM, QUESTIONS AND EXPLORES.	VERY GOOD AT NETWORKING POSITIVE, CHEERFUL, SUSTAINS THE TEAM.	LACKS SELF DISCIPLINE, IMPULSIVE, QUICK TO LOSE INTEREST.
MONITOR EVALUATOR	CRITICAL THINKER, ANALYSES IDEAS, CONSTANTLY REVIEWS THE TEAM.	INTERPRETS COMPLEX DATA JUDGEMENT, HARD-HEADED OBJECTIVE.	OVER CRITICAL, NEGATIVE, INTELLECTUALLY COMPETITIVE, SCEPTICAL & CYNICAL.
TEAM WORKER	SOCIALLY ORIENTATED, LOYAL TO THE TEAM, PROMOTES HARMONY, PERCEPTIVE OF FEELINGS, NEEDS AND CONCERNS.	STABLE, EXTROVERT, GOOD LISTENER, PROMOTES STRENGTHS, UNDERPINS WEAKNESSES.	INDECISIVE, CAN FORGET A TASK.
COMPLETER FINISHER	DRIVES FOR TASK COMPLETION ON TIME AND ACCORDING TO SPECIFICATION.	OBSESSED WITH DETAIL, STRONG SENSE OF PURPOSE DRIVEN BY TARGETS.	ANXIOUS, COMPULSIVE, CAN LOWER MORALE.

Figure 8.5 Belbin's team roles

A person's team characteristics are identified on the basis of completing a diagnostic inventory. This will usually identify one or two roles that score significantly higher than others, i.e. are likely to be the dominant types of behaviour. Other types will receive very low scores and are probably not available. The interpretation of individual results needs to bear a number of points in mind:

- there are no 'right or wrong' or 'good or bad' types – all are valid and appropriate;
- the balance of the scoring will probably indicate a range of possible team behaviours;
- the scoring will reflect the types in a given context at a certain time, both factors are variable and scoring can change;
- the secondary type can often be developed.

Although the Belbin inventory provides the basis for useful personal insights and self-appraisal it is even more powerful if used by a whole team as the basis for analysis of the team's working patterns. This can be a useful exercise at the forming stage. Consider a team that is made up of three shapers, one chair and a company worker. It is more than likely that the storming stage will reach hurricane proportions as the majority of the team will be striving to be dominant and the company worker will have a very negative experience. If status is added into the equation then the chances are that the team's inability to function will lead to decisions being made outside the team and imposed.

The converse example is also problematic – a team that is composed of company and team workers with perhaps a resource investigator is just as likely to fail to achieve its task. A further issue for schools is that (on the basis of observation rather than systematic research) many teams in schools lack monitor evaluators and completer finishers. This has significant implications for teams being able to complete tasks on time and according to specification.

The effective team, the quality team, is one that balances team roles so that task completion and the process issues are balanced. There can be no prescription for the ideal or optimum team but there do seem to be some guide-lines:

- there should be one chair or one shaper, not both;
- according to the size of the team there should be a balance of team and company workers;
- other types should be included according to the nature of the task.

The senior management team of a highly regarded secondary school has the following make-up:

Post	Primary role	Secondary role
Head	Resource investigator	Chair
Deputy (Curriculum)	Company worker	Shaper
Deputy (Pastoral)	Chair	Team worker
Senior teacher (Admin)	Completer finisher	Company worker
Senior teacher (TVEI)	Team worker	Resources investigator

More by luck than planning the school is led by a team that has a range of complementary roles with secondary roles that allow for flexibility according to circumstance. Research in a primary school revealed that the head was a shaper/team worker and all her staff were company/team workers. Harmony reigned but the burden on the head was enormous. A working party on appraisal in a secondary school failed perhaps because the designated chair was a company worker, the other members of the group were either shapers or innovators and there was no completer finisher or monitor evaluator.

Belbin's work is problematic – the inventory was not designed for use in the education sector, his types derived from a study of small groups on management courses and the scientific validity of his research has yet to be fully tested. However, his work has met with a high degree of acceptance and it does provide the starting point for detailed and systematic analysis. In the context of team building the Belbin inventory can help by:

- providing data for the analysis of team working and so facilitating discussion;
- indicating possible causes of failure and potential remedies;
- acting as a dispassionate means of discussing individual behaviour;
- identifying the composition of a team and so informing team development needs;
- helping with recruitment of team members when other appropriate factors have been taken into account;
- diagnosing individual development needs;
- identifying factors in team success, so allowing them to be replicated.

Team building is too complex to be left to serendipity. There are undoubtedly many successful teams – but perhaps they could be better. Time is too precious to accept unsatisfactory teams as inevitable, team membership being a crucial determinant of an individual's perception of work. Quality criteria therefore need to be applied to make teams quality experiences.

Team development

Effective teams result from empowered individuals learning to collaborate so that individual knowledge, skills and qualities are deployed to maximum effect. The group is one of the most powerful learning vehicles so the effective team has the potential to heighten the learning of its members if its standard operating procedures are perceived as learning opportunities. This involves an understanding of:

- how teams learn;
- what they need to learn;
- what techniques are appropriate.

Teams learn by relating experience to analysis and changing behaviour in the future (see Figure 8.6).

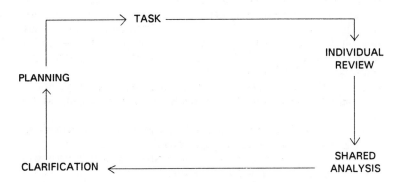

Figure 8.6   How teams learn (West-Burnham 1990)

Having completed a task individual members of the team review their own behaviour, that of their colleagues and of the team as a whole both in terms of task achievement and team processes. These individual perceptions are then shared and a consensus view of the team's performance emerges: problems are identified, reasons for failure established and the factors involved in success celebrated and reinforced. This allows the team to clarify, to understand its behaviour, and so agree how to approach the next task, what behaviour to stress, what to minimise so as to improve its performance. Three vital functions are taking place in this process.

1. The team is learning from direct, real experience – the most powerful learning agent.
2. The team is looking to continuously improve its performance.
3. The learning process is part of the work process – there is no artificial divide in terms of significance or loss of work time.

Two changes in team management are necessary to create a learning team. Firstly, time has to be built in to the team's activities to allow for planning and review; in essence this means that review becomes an agenda item. Secondly, this review needs to be detailed and systematic ensuring that every team member feels able to contribute fully. This implies a range of skills that need to be developed.

The components of effective teams identified in Figure 8.1 provide the context from which team training needs can be identified. In many ways the list corresponds to any portfolio of management development activities. The crucial difference is that the training is for the team as an entity and not in piecemeal form for the individuals in it. Too many team development courses are attended by individuals representing the team – this inevitably compromises the impact and integrity of the training. The team that trains together develops together.

The skills appropriate to effective team working are set out in Figure 8.7. This list might appear somewhat intimidating unless it is recognised that:

-   teams will not work effectively without them ('If you think training's expensive, try ignorance!');
-   they are generic skills and will transfer into a wide variety of situations, notably the classroom.

LISTENING	COLLABORATING DECISION MAKING
QUESTIONING	PROBLEM SOLVING
GIVING FEEDBACK	CONFLICT RESOLUTION
SUMMARISING	TIME MANAGEMENT
PROPOSING IDEAS	STRESS MANAGEMENT
BUILDING ON SUGGESTIONS	MANAGING MEETINGS
BEING OPEN ABOUT FEELINGS	PUBLIC SPEAKING
ASSERTIVENESS	WRITTEN COMMUNICATION

Figure 8.7   Skills for effective team work

The methods that are appropriate to the development of these skills are widely understood but not always applied:

1.   The team must train and learn together.
2.   It is often easier to start the process away from the work place.

3. Consultants/facilitators can drive the process and help keep the focus.
4. Non-threatening activities – the notorious management games, are often the best way to start.
5. Outdoor team development can be very powerful, instructive and fun.
6. The training should be designed by team members on the basis of perceived need.
7. The training should focus on the issues of implementation.
8. The initial event should be seen as the start of the learning process, not the process itself.
9. Team activities subsequent to the training should make constant reference to the lessons learnt.
10. The skills and expertise of team members must be used as a permanent resource.

Team training and development activities are rather like circling the earth in a space shuttle. The angle of re-entry is crucial – too steep (or enthusiastic) and the team is burnt up in the rich atmosphere of colleagues' cynicism; too shallow and the team bounces off the atmosphere, doomed to circle the real world and become management consultants. Training works if it is manifested in behaviour – there is no other justification for it.

Quality circles

The quality circle movement is one of the most frequently cited manifestations of total quality management. The movement emerged in Japan in the early 1960s and has been used across the world as a major strategy to involve 'shop floor' and production workers in a drive for quality. The primary motivations behind the movement have been to create a sense of involvement and ownership and to strengthen the feeling of workers as crafts people. An immediate question has to be raised about the applicability of such a technique to professionals who are working in teams, however immature those teams might be.

The key characteristics of quality circles are:

– between 3 and 12 members;
– people doing the same job or process;
– attendance is voluntary;
– meetings are regular, perhaps one hour per week;
– meetings take place in working time;
– they are led by the 'supervisor';

- they identify, analyse and propose solutions to work based problems;
- they recommend solutions to management;
- they implement those solutions.

The crucial thing about quality circles is that they are trained in the use of analytical problem solving methods so that those with responsibility for making a process work are directly involved in the improvement of that process – their experience is respected and their solutions are implemented. The quality circle movement has probably had as many failures as successes, the latter being mainly due to a lack of commitment, inadequate training and a lack of seriousness on the part of management.

There is little doubt that quality circles provide a useful model, most importantly in the transfer of responsibility to those who actually have to do the work. Their voluntary nature is clearly problematic and it would be nonsense to diffuse limited time and energy by having teams and quality circles in parallel. There may well be a case for arguing that the approach is valid for non-teaching staff given their different contracts of employment; however, this implies an unacceptable hierarchy of quality which would clearly be inappropriate and counter-productive. The answer would seem to be to combine the principles of effective quality circles to create what Peters (1988) calls 'self-managing teams'. In essence self-managing teams have high degrees of autonomy – everyone is a member of a team of 8–15, teams assume direct responsibility for much of their workload and there is very limited specialisation within teams. Individual appraisal and pay are limited to the team's work.

The detailed implications of this approach have already been discussed in Chapter 6, but it is worth restating the issue of hierarchy, the role of middle management in a team environment and the importance of consistency in a total quality environment.

Summary

- A team is a quality group and quality programmes depend on effective team-work.
- Teams in schools are often teams in name only.
- Effective teams display nine key characteristics.
- Clear values, pride and appropriate leadership are pre-requisites to effective team working.
- Teams cannot operate without a clear task, regular feedback and review, and openness and candour.

- Team processes involve lateral communication, collaborative decision making and outcomes in terms of action.
- Effective teams balance task and process.
- Team building requires awareness of the stages of team development and the factors influencing individual behaviour.
- Team development involves seeing learning as a crucial component of team activity.
- Teamwork requires a range of generic skills.
- Quality circles are not an alternative to teams but provide an alternative perspective.
- Effective teams may well mature into self-managing teams with significant implications for roles and school structures.

Action

- Review any team of which you are a member in terms of:
  - its ability to get things done;
  - its social maturity;
  - its use of training and development.

- For any team for which you are leader:

  - plan the introduction of review sessions;
  - analyse the extent to which you have empowered team members;
  - review your own team role.

- Look at the way in which teams work outside school. What can you learn from them?
- Agree a plan of action to make your team a quality team.

9 Implementation

This chapter outlines and discusses some of the issues associated with the implementation of TQM in a school. Four key issues need to be to the forefront of any implementation strategy:

1. 'Just do it!' This was the reported response of Deming to repeated requests for advice on implementation. Although brief to the point of obscurity it contains a vital message: action is more important than analysis. There is a great danger of over-intellectualising the process.
2. A long-term view is needed; TQM is about attitudes and these are not moved by exhortation or lecture. In many organisations it has taken three to five years to be confident that a quality culture has been created. On the other hand there are very simple and direct actions that can be taken that will have an immediate impact.
3. More organisations have failed to implement TQM than have successfully implemented it. The reason is usually a lack of commitment and a failure to appreciate the totality of the impact on an organisation. Piecemeal involvement is doomed.
4. The implementation process must be seen as a quality process in its own right. Those who are responsible for managing the implementation must use quality processes and techniques. The credibility of TQM will be determined by the sensitivity of its implementation.

This chapter will examine the principal components of the implementation process:

- management commitment;

- driving the process;
- review;
- strategy;
- training;
- structures and systems;
- management behaviour;
- continuous improvement.

Fundamental to these eight points is the management of change. It is not appropriate in this context to review all the issues associated with managing change. However, two principles are worth stressing. Fullan (1981) argues that real change involves dealing with attitudes and values and therefore change has to be about learning. Joyce and Showers (1981) argue that real learning only takes place when a range of criteria are met – most importantly the notion of feedback on performance. Effective learning (and by extension, effective change) must therefore be firmly rooted in the work place and management relationships need to have development at their heart.

Management commitment

TQM will only work if there is explicit single minded and obsessive commitment to quality. Any hint of compromise or reservation will diminish the credibility of the implementation strategy. The importance of vision in leadership has already been stressed; equally important is the way that the vision is communicated and the way that it is demonstrated in action.

The specific requirements on managers are clear:

- to develop and display consistency of purpose, i.e. to speak with one voice;
- to implement quality procedures in all aspects of their work – especially team development and problem solving/decision making techniques;
- to engage in training and development activities;
- to recognise that many quality problems are the result of management action;
- to ensure that resources are made available;
- to talk and act quality;
- to manage the implementation of TQM as a high priority.

In essence quality should not be an 'agenda item' but permeate every issue. The question to be asked of every issue is 'What are the quality implications of our response to this...?'

The chapters on leadership and teams in this book have identified a range of skills appropriate to quality management. Long before senior managers presume to introduce TQM they should review their own preparedness and take appropriate action. The most important single determinant of the success of an implementation strategy is the behaviour of senior managers. Actions which are incompatible with the quality approach, language which implies scepticism or cynicism will inevitably diminish credibility and create cynicism. Once initiated quality cannot be compartmentalised – it must permeate all aspects of school leadership and management.

Driving the process

Although quality is everyone's responsibility it is necessary to identify an individual and a team specifically responsible for driving the implementation process in school. Commercial organisations usually appoint a TQM manager or facilitator. Schools cannot afford the luxury of a specific appointment but there is a need to designate a named individual to have responsibility for managing implementation. There are three criteria for such an appointment – authority to make decisions, knowledge of TQM, and enthusiasm and commitment. The specific responsibilities of such a post might include:

- promoting the total quality approach;
- acting as internal consultant to teams;
- advising managers on operational issues;
- designing and delivering training;
- liaising with external suppliers and customers;
- communicating progress to all staff;
- monitoring and evaluating the implementation process.

In essence the role of the facilitator is to make TQM live, to help all colleagues translate the theory into practice. However, the task is a major one and probably too much for one individual. It may therefore be appropriate to eatablish a quality team, a task team with the specific purpose of making TQM happen. Whatever the constitution of the team it should never be allowed to detract from the fact that every team has to be a quality team and the creation of a specific team should not allow others to abrogate responsibility for quality in its own sphere of activity. The existence of a 'quality team' can create inertia elsewhere.

The team's most appropriate functions are probably:

- to provide advice and support to the facilitator;
- to act as a model of effective team working;
- to integrate TQM with other school initiatives;
- to pilot specific strategies;
- to generate resources to support implementation;
- to act as a forum for generating commitment;
- to disseminate ideas and experience.

Two intangibles are vital to the quality facilitator and team; an infectious enthusiasm for quality and high levels of personal integrity.

Review

In Chapter 1 review was established as a key link between TQM and the school effectiveness and improvement movements. Analysis of the current situation is the essential precursor to any quality initiative. Without a systematic review the strategy may be misdirected and inappropriate and more importantly key strengths may be ignored and thereby not integrated.

The main purpose of the review is to establish what is to be changed, i.e. to analyse the existing situation in quality terms. Such a review should be initiated and managed by the quality facilitator and might well follow the form of the inventory at the end of Chapter 1. The content and structure of the review should be determined by the context, audience and possible applications of the outcomes. Thus a range of review documents may be necessary, aimed at:

- children;
- parents;
- teaching and non-teaching staff;
- external agencies, e.g. the LEA, other schools etc.

Whatever the audience the central issues remain the same:

- current levels of satisfaction;
- the extent to which needs are being met;
- how the school compares with other schools;
- identification of areas of waste;
- identification of areas of non-conformance;
- suggestions for improvement.

The results of this review process will help to identify the priorities to be taken into account in planning the strategy. The inventories can also be used at a later date to allow measurement of changes in levels of satisfaction, i.e. the extent to which the TQM process is actually changing the way the school is managed. Two important principles are established by the use of reviews; *listening* to customers at the very outset and *measuring* changing levels of satisfaction. The design of the review sheets should allow for quantifications of results.

The major caution with the review process is that once it is started it will raise expectations that will have to be met. Failure to act on the outcomes will almost certainly exacerbate existing concerns and create disillusionment.

Strategy

Once the personnel to manage implementation have been identified and the priorities have been established then it is appropriate to identify the specific strategy. Although the implementation of TQM has to be seen as a specific initiative it should not be divorced from school management processes. It should not be seen as a 'what?' but rather as a 'how?'. It would therefore be appropriate to integrate the TQM strategy into the school development plan. The plan is necessary to provide a clear view of the path to be followed and to act as a quality criterion, a benchmark to monitor progress as well as acting as a constant reminder of the central purpose. The development plan needs to include the following elements:

Mission statement

Existing school aims and 'objectives' need to be integrated into a mission statement as outlined in Chapter 5. The important change is in the language which should reflect the shift to customer satisfaction through quality processes. At this stage it is vital that the desired culture and values are made explicit and articulated into the mission statement.

Objectives

The mission statement should be translated into specific objectives which indicate the outcomes to be achieved in a specified time-scale. These objectives should have the following characteristics:

- success criteria are identified;
- time-scale is specified;

- responsibility is delegated;
- resources are allocated;
- teams and individuals are specified.

These objectives will form the basis of personal target setting through the appraisal process. The objectives should relate to the specific components of implementation, notably training and organisation.

Organisation

The review will have indicated specific issues relating to the organisation of the school. Central to this will be the extent to which existing structures are compatible with the notion of quality teams. The plan should indicate the processes for transforming existing structures and working procedures into suitable vehicles for managing quality.

Where appropriate there should be reconsideration of decision-making structures so as to facilitate the adoption of a quality approach. These issues have been discussed in detail in Chapter 6. The development plan should indicate the specific measures to be adopted in a particular school.

Training and development

This is so central and significant that a move towards TQM cannot be contemplated without it. The issue is dealt with in more detail below but certain principles can be stated as fundamental:

- every stage of the implementation process should be accompanied by training;
- everyone should be trained;
- training should cover the spectrum of skills;
- the training programme should be based on a process of needs analysis.

The development plan should indicate the training priorities for implementing TQM, the methods of needs analysis to be employed, the means of delivery and the resources available.

Resources

The implementation strategy needs to be costed both in terms of financial expenditure and staff time. As with all educational activities many aspects of the management process will be difficult to cost.

However, it is essential that an attempt is made in order to allow for prioritising in the budget and to demonstrate commitment.

It is also important to view expenditure on implementing TQM as an investment from which there may not be immediate returns. The most significant item of expenditure will be staff time, but the criterion to be applied is that of opportunity cost – what will happen if significant change is not implemented?

Success criteria

Integral to the development plan should be success criteria to allow progress to be measured. These should be as specific as possible and quantified where appropriate. One of the most important criteria will relate to the use of attitudinal surveys to measure the impact of the quality programme.

The success criteria should also relate to specific changes to be introduced and failure to meet targets should be examined using the tools identified in Chapter 4.

Training

The success of implementing TQM depends on training because the success of the process depends fundamentally on attitudinal change. At the same time making the total quality approach work requires the application of very specific skills and procedures. Training has to be seen as an integral component of managing quality – it is not a parallel or even a support process but a fundamental component. Continuous improvement means continuous development and the principles of right first time and conformity to requirements are particularly appropriate. The following principles should apply:

- Training and development should be specific to the school and not 'off the shelf'; the 'language' of training should grow out of the school's mission.
- Trainers, consultants and training materials should work to the specific needs of the school; customer needs must be stated.
- Training should not be restricted to attending courses or 'training days', all meetings and activities should be examined for their training potential.
- Training activities should be designed to include feedback – coaching is an essential component to ensure that there is genuine change.

The training programme needs to include a wide range of topics; some specific to TQM, others of a broader applicability. The contents of a training strategy might include:

- introduction to the principles of TQM;
- identification of the need to change;
- raising the issue of customer awareness;
- analysis of work processes;
- application of quantitative and analytical techniques;
- team building skills;
- leadership skills;
- interpersonal skills, notably listening and feedback;
- oral and written communication and presentation skills;
- review and debriefing skills.

Many of these skills will already be present in schools, or will have been developed in other contexts; It is most important that extant skills are recognised and reinforced. Another very important issue is the training and awareness raising to be made available to children, parents, governors and others who come into regular contact with the school. At the very least they need to be informed; at best a strategy will be developed to integrate them fully into the school's scheme.

One of the great potential strengths of TQM in schools is the development of the approach by children. They are clearly a vital source of feedback but also essential protagonists in making classrooms and schools quality environments. Most children have considerable skills in articulating their requirements, many adolescents are 'natural customers'. A school cannot claim to be a quality organisation unless all those with whom it comes into contact are integrated into quality processes and this includes training.

Training is too often regarded as a cost rather than an investment. One of the major problems is that training has direct costs (course fees, consultant charges etc.) and indirect costs (teachers not teaching, managers not managing). If the TQM approach is to be fully integrated into a school then training and development must not be seen as separate activities but a natural component of all interactions. Departmental meetings become opportunities for team development – 'discussions' can be developed into coaching; everybody in a position of responsibility is expected to develop colleagues as an essential component of their job.

Structures and systems

This is perhaps one of the most fundamental challenges to schools. Chapter 6 has identified the issues in terms of developing a quality structure and it would be wrong to underestimate the difficulties in changing a school's structure. The most significant difficulty is the inherited distribution of posts which cannot be abandoned overnight. Operating relationships and the concept of succession planning can be introduced to move the school's structure towards the desired format.

What can be done very rapidly is to enhance existing structures by refocusing and realigning their working procedures. In essence by converting departments into teams, by changing meetings into problem solving and creative activities. This change can take place with minimal cost and disruption and can produce a dramatic impact on motivation, involvement and satisfaction.

More complex but equally vital is the realignment of systems. In practical terms this means establishing customer requirements and then recording them in such a way as to ensure consistency and conformity. In practical terms this means producing codified operating procedures which define in significant detail the components of a process so that there is no ambiguity. Almost every aspect of a school's work is capable of being codified except the essential element – what Handy (1990) refers to as the intangibles – and these cannot and must not be codified. It is not intended to advocate 'behaviour codes' requiring a standardised greeting with a regulation smile to greet 30 disaffected adolescents first thing on a Monday morning. (Even though many of those young people will be subject to such a code on Saturdays when at work!)

What can be codified is the core of a process, the essentials: examples of school activities appropriate to such an approach include:

- job descriptions;
- syllabuses and schemes of work;
- procedures relating to attendance;
- review and reporting procedures;
- appraisal and staff development;
- marking criteria;
- homework procedures;
- uniform;
- health and safety;
- time tabling;
- record keeping;

- option procedures;
- records of achievement;
- development planning;
- budget planning;
- stock control.

Many of these activities are routine but all impact on customers and, if efficiently managed, can create time for more specifically educational activities – most importantly communication with children, parents and colleagues. It is only through codification that quality can be guaranteed – as long as it is customer requirements that are codified and not bureaucratic routines.

Management behaviour

The responsibilities of leadership have been discussed in Chapter 7. However, it is worth reiterating the importance of consistency during the implementation phase. If TQM is not to be dismissed as another management 'fad', as the result of another course or even the outcome of reading a book then certain attributes are essential:

– Consistency	This means all managers, in all situations delivering the same message. The senior management team must speak with one voice and act with one purpose.
– Enthusiasm	It is easy to ridicule the 'enthusiast' but real change will be directly proportionate to expressed commitment.
– Attention to detail	Every aspect of work must be noted, successes reinforced and praised, problems solved and weaknesses and lapses picked up.
– Listening	Constantly listening – remembering always that we have two eyes, two ears and one mouth and that ratio sends an important message to quality managers.
– Accessibility	Being available, constantly on the ground, managing by walking about (MBWA).

In the final analysis quality management comes down to performance and relationships and managers have to display the highest standards of integrity in both at all times.

Continuous improvement

Although it is essential to have a clear strategy for the implementation of TQM it would be a mistake to see it as a separate process. It needs to be seen as the start of a process of continuous improvement in which there is a continuous challenging of norms and expectations. TQM implicitly denies the possibility that any organisation or individual has reached a plateau which represents an acceptable level of performance. Implementing TQM requires the acceptance of the principle that 'We can always improve' and although the gradient may lessen, going up is the only direction for a TQM school.

In practice this means constantly checking, redefining and improving. Schools are the most natural organisations for this culture as they are already expert in managing the most complex improvement process of all: the moral, intellectual, social and personal development of children.

Summary

- Plan, act, review.

Action

- 'Just do it!'

Appendix BS 5750

Most readers will be familiar with the British Standards kitemark and will probably use it as a criterion when selecting goods for purchase. It is clear proof that a product conforms to clear standards for safety, reliability and quality. In essence the presence of the kitemark reassures the buyer that the goods are fit for the purpose intended. BS 5750 is the kitemark for quality management systems; it is directly replicated as International Standard ISO 9000 and European Standard EN 29000.

BS 5750 is not total quality management, the two are not synonymous and should not be confused. BS 5750 is a very powerful vehicle for ensuring that key organisational processes are being managed in a consistent manner and achieve conformance to a given or implied specification. The standard is used as the basis for certification of an organisation following an assessment audit carried out by an accredited third party certification body. Confirmation of the award of BS 5750 status is subject to frequent review.

A very large number of organisations now use the standard as the basis for managing quality systems. Its origins lie in engineering but the standard has been gradually developed so that it now covers the full range of production and service organisations. In recent years there has been growing interest in the public sector, notably the health service and further education. This is partly in response to potential employers who wish to deal with certified suppliers and partly in response to the Training Agency and Training and Enterprise Councils who are adopting quality management practices. In response to this demand the BSI has prepared guidance notes for education and training.

The factors which schools might consider in reviewing the relevance of BS 5750 are:

1. It is increasingly becoming the 'language' of industry, commerce and the public sector.
2. Certification is a public demonstration of an organisation's commitment to quality.
3. The organisation retains full responsibility for the management of processes.
4. It is 'content free', i.e. it does not prescribe what an organisation should do but rather helps to ensure consistency of delivery.
5. It provides the basis for developing quality management systems by identifying the irreducible minimum.
6. The organisation retains responsibility for setting standards and measuring performance.

BS 5750 identifies four key factors of a quality system:

1. Management responsibility.
2. Personnel and resources.
3. Quality systems.
4. Interface with customers.

Each of these can in turn be broken down into key components:

1. Management responsibility
   1.1 A quality policy which defines the key characteristics of the service to be provided.
   1.2 Quality objectives which translate the policy into specific objectives.
   1.3 Responsibility and authority structures to ensure that the objectives are met.
   1.4 Management review procedures to ensure that the quality system is operating as intended.

2. Personnel and resources
   2.1 Individual motivation should be recognised through selection, recognition and reward systems and by creating involvement in all aspects of work.
   2.2 Training and development which enhances the capacity of individuals to operate quality systems.
   2.3 Communication should be a major feature for all aspects of the organisation.
   2.4 Resources should be provided appropriate to the specific operations required.

3. Quality systems
    3.1 Quality systems should be established to control all processes. The emphasis should be on prevention.
    3.2 Quality feedback from customers should be identified through the service quality loop.
    3.3 Documentation should be produced including a quality manual, plan, procedures and records.
    3.4 Internal quality audits should be performed to verify the implementation and effectiveness of quality systems.
4. Interface with customers
    4.1 Management should establish mechanisms to ensure responsiveness to customer needs.
    4.2 Processes should be established to ensure effective two-way communication with customers.

The above is a very limited account of BS 5750 in relation to services. Further work has been done in developing the model to apply to education and training in general and it may well be that specific work is required with regard to schools. Although the way in which the standard is expressed may be alien to many schools in fact (as argued in Chapters 3, 4 and 9 above) many of the process structures and documentation already exist in schools. It is a matter of integrating any systemising in order to ensure consistency. A parallel may be drawn with managing a school's finances. An accounting system is essential to monitor income and expenditure, – chaos would result without it. BS 5750 is a structured approach to managing quality which actually simplifies and clarifies, so creating time.

BS 5750 is not TQM; most notably it does not refer in detail to some of the crucial components of TQM:

– Continuous improvement.
– Leadership.
– Team work.
– Driving out fear.
– Measurement of variation.
– Breaking down barriers.
– Constancy of purpose.
– Vision.

This does not mean that BS 5750 is inadequate or incomplete, rather that it needs to be set in a TQM context in order for its full potential to be realised. What BS 5750 does do is provide the basis for managing the system, TQM provides the context. The standard deals with the core, TQM with the intangibles – both are valid and significant and mutually supportive. Each is compromised in the absence of the other.

Further information on BS 5750 is available from BSI, Linford Wood, Milton Keynes MK14 6LE.

References

Adair, J. 1986 *Effective Teambuilding* Gower.

Adair, J. 1988 *Developing Leaders: The Ten Key Principles* The Talbot Adair Press.

Adair, J. 1990 *The Challenge of Innovation* The Talbot Adair Press.

Atkinson, P.E. 1990 *Creating Culture Change: The Key to Successful Total Quality Management* IFS Ltd, UK.

Belbin R.M. 1981 *Management Teams: Why they Succeed or Fail* Heinemann.

Blake, R.R. and Mouton, J.S. 1964 *The Managerial Grid* Gulf Publishing Co.

Blake, R.R. and Mouton, J.S. 1978 *The New Managerial Grid* Gulf Publishing Co.

Bone, D. and Griggs, R. 1989 *Quality at Work* Kogan Page, Crisp Pub. Inc.

Brown, A. 1990 *Customer Care Management* Heinemann Professional Pub. Ltd.

Byham, W.C. (with J. Cox) 1991 *Zapp! The Lightning of Empowerment* Business Books Ltd, Random Century.

Campbell, A. and Tawadey, K. 1990 *Mission and Business Philosophy: Winning Employee Commitment* Heinemann Professional Pub. Ltd.

Clutterbuck, D. and Crainer, S. 1990 *Makers of Management: Men and Women who changed the Business World* Guild Publishing.

Collard, R. 1989 *Total Quality: Success Through People* Institute of Personal Management.

Crosby, P.B. 1979 *Quality is Free* McGraw-Hill.

Crosby, P.B. 1986 *Quality Without Tears: The Art of Hassle-Free Management* McGraw-Hill Book Co., Singapore.

Dale, B.G. and Plunkett, J.J. (ed.) 1990 *Managing Quality* Philip Allan.

Davies, B., Ellison, L., Osborne, A. and West-Burnham, J. 1990 *Education Management for the 1990s* Longman Group UK.

Deming, W.E. 1986 *Out of the Crisis* M.I.T. Center for Advanced Engineering Study.

D.E.S., 1989 *School Teacher Appraisal: A National Framework* Report of the National Steering Group H.M.S.O.

D.E.S, 1991 'School Teacher Appraisal', Circular 12/91.

D.T.I., *Standards, Quality and International Competitiveness* CMND 8621.

Dyer, W.G. 1987 *Team Building: Issues and Alternatives* 2nd edn, Addison-Wesley Pub.

Everard, B. and Morris, G. 1990 *Effective School Management* 2nd edn, Paul Chapman Ltd.

Feigenbaum, A.V. 1987 *Total Quality Control* McGraw-Hill.

Fraser-Robinson, J. (with Mosscrop, P.) 1991 *Total Quality Marketing* Kogan Page.

Fullan, M. 1982 *The Meaning of Educational Change* Teachers College Press.

Fullan, M. 1985 'Change processes and strategies at the local level' *Elementary School Journal* 85, 3.

Goldsmith, W. and Clutterbuck, D. 1984 *The Winning Streak* George Weidenfield & Nicolson.

Gray, J. and Starke, F. 1988 *Organisational Behaviour: Concepts and Applications* 4th edn, Merrill.

Hall, V., Mackay, H. and Morgan, C. 1986 *Head Teachers at Work* Open University Press.

Handy, C. 1989 *The Age of Unreason* Business Books; Arrow.

Handy, C. 1990 *Inside Organisations: 21 Ideas for Managers* BBC Books.

Hayes, R. and Abernathy W.J. 1980 'Managing our way to economic decline' *Harvard Business Review* Jul/Aug.

Hickman, C.R. 1991 and Silva, M.A. 1984 *Creating Excellence: Managing Corporate Culture Strategy and Change in the New Age* George Allen and Unwin.

Hodson, P. 1987 'Managers can be taught but leaders have to learn' *ICT* Nov/Dec.

Honey, P. 1988 *Improve your People Skills* Institute of Personal Management, London.

Hopkins, D. 1987 *Improving the Quality of Schooling* Falmer Press.

Horovitz, J. 1990 *How to Win Customers: Using Customer Service for a Competitive Edge* Pitman.

Hutchins, D. 1990 *In Pursuit of Quality: Participative Techniques for Quality Improvement* Pitman.

Ishikawa, K. 1976 *Guide to Quality Control* Asian Productivity Organisation.

Jenkins, H.O. 1991 *Getting it Right: A Handbook for Successful School Leadership* Basil Blackwell.

Joyce, B. and Showers, B. 1980 'Improving In-Service Training' *Education Leadership* Vol. 37.

Juran, J.M. 1979 *Quality Control Handbook* McGraw-Hill.

Kanter, R.M. 1984 *The Change Masters* Allen & Unwin.

Kanter, R.M. 1989 *When Giants Learn to Dance* Simon & Schuster.

Lessem, R. 1985 *The Roots of Excellence* Fontana Paperbacks.

Lessem, R. 1991 *Total Quality Learning: Building a Learning Organisation* Basil Blackwell.

Likert, R. 1961 *New Patterns of Management* McGraw-Hill.

MacDonald, J. and Piggott, J. 1990 *Global Quality: The New Management Culture* Mercury.

Martin, W.B. 1989 *Managing Quality Customer Service* Kogan Page.

Mastenbroek, W. (ed.) 1991 *Managing for Quality in the Service Sector* Basil Blackwell.

McGregor, D. 1960 *The Human Side of Enterprise* McGraw-Hill.

Murgatroyd, S. 1985 'Management Teams and the Promotion of Staff Well Being *School Organisation* Vol. 6, No. 1.

Oakland, J.S. 1989 *Total Quality Management* Heinemann Professional Pub. Ltd.

Peters, T. 1988 *Thriving on Chaos: Handbook for a Management Revolution* Guild Publishing.

Peters, T. and Austin, N. 1985 *A Passion for Excellence* Collins.

Peters T.J. and Waterman, 1982 *In Search of Excellence* Harper & Row.

Sallis, E. 1991 *Total Quality Management and Further Education* Paper presented at the BEMAS Conference 1991.

Schon, D.A. 1983 *The Reflective Practitioner: How Professionals Think in Action* Basic Books.

Schonberger, R.J. 1990 *Building a Chain of Customers: Linking Business Functions to Create the World Class Company* Guild Publishing.

Sieff, M. 1988 *Don't Ask The Price* Fontana Paperbacks.

Sieff, M. 1991 *Management the Marks and Spencer Way* Fontana Paperbacks.

Stewart, V. 1990 *The David Solution: How to Reclaim Power and Liberate your Organisation* Crower.

Taguchi, G. 1981 *On-line Quality Control during Production* Japanese Standards Association.

Torrington, D., Weightman, J. and Johns, K. 1989 *Effective Management: People and Organisation* Prentice Hall International.

Torrington, D., Weightman, J. and Johns, K. 1989 *The Reality of School Management* Basil Blackwell.

Tuckman, B.W. 1985 'Development Sequence in Small Groups' *Psychological Bulletin* Vol. 63.

Webb, I. 1991 *Quest for Quality* The Industrial Society.

West-Burnham, J. 1990 'Human Resource Management' in Davies, B. (*op. cit*).

Whiteley, R.C. 1991 *The Customer Driven Company: Moving from Talk to Action* The Forum Corporation, Addison-Wesley.

Review

You, the reader, are my customer. In order to be consistent with the approaches advocated in this book, I need feedback from you. Would you therefore please complete and return the following review to me? Please ring the number that reflects your view.

1. The book met my expectations:
   Strongly disagree   1 2 3 4 5 6 7   Strongly agree
2. The book is relevant and practical:
   Strongly disagree   1 2 3 4 5 6 7   Strongly agree
3. The language and tone of the book are appropriate:
   Strongly disagree   1 2 3 4 5 6 7   Strongly agree
4. The structure and organisation of the book are helpful:
   Strongly disagree   1 2 3 4 5 6 7   Strongly agree
5. I can apply the strategies outlined in the book:
   Strongly disagree   1 2 3 4 5 6 7   Strongly agree
6. The book has helped develop my thinking about quality:
   Strongly disagree   1 2 3 4 5 6 7   Strongly agree

Any other comments on the book?

Any comments on the issue of quality in schools?

Thank you for your time. Please return this questionnaire to:

> John West-Burnham
> QEd
> 6A Bird Street
> Lichfield
> Staffs

I would also be very interested to hear of schools implementing TQM and BS 5750. Any information would be gratefully received and used to help establish a network of TQM schools. Please send details to the above address. Requests for training and consultancy may also be directed to QEd.

Index